D0948340

DATE DUE

NIGERIA

OUR LATEST PROTECTORATE

HAUSA CONTINGENT, UNDER MAJOR J. A. BURDON, WHICH TOOK PART IN THE JUBILEE PROCESSION.

NIGERIA Our Latest Protectorate

By Charles Henry Robinson M.A

CANON MISSIONER OF RIPON AND LECTURER IN HAUSA
IN THE UNIVERSITY OF CAMBRIDGE

WITH MAP AND ILLUSTRATIONS

NEGRO UNIVERSITIES PRESS
NEW YORK

Originally published in 1900
by Horace Marshall and Son

Reprinted 1969 by
Negro Universities Press
A DIVISION OF GREENWOOD PUBLISHING CORP.
NEW YORK

SBN 8371-1542-6

PRINTED IN UNITED STATES OF AMERICA

INTRODUCTION

NO introduction is required for this description of the latest addition to the British Empire, except for the sake of affording me the opportunity of thanking those who have so kindly assisted to illustrate it. I am indebted to the Rt. Hon. Sir Geo. Goldie for permission to use several photographs taken in connection with the work of the Royal Niger Company, also to Dr. W. H. Crosse, for many years Medical Officer of the Company, for the loan of many photographs taken by himself, and to Miss C. M. Stiff, of Cheltenham, for preparing several drawings of native articles.   To those whose interest may be aroused by a perusal of this book in the well‑being of the peoples of Nigeria, I would specially commend the concluding paragraph of the chapter on the Hausa Association.

C. H. R.

Ripon, *February* 1, 1900

CONTENTS

Chapter I

INTRODUCTORY

Chapter II

ORIGIN OF THE HAUSA PEOPLE

Chapter III

THE HAUSA SOLDIER

Chapter IV

AMONGST THE HAUSAS

CONTENTS

Chapter V

THE DAY'S MARCH

Chapter VI

TRAVELLING IN NIGERIA

Chapter VII

THE ROYAL NIGER COMPANY

Chapter VIII

MISSIONARY ENTERPRISE IN NIGERIA

CONTENTS

Chapter IX

THE HAUSA ASSOCIATION

Chapter X

A WALK THROUGH THE KANO MARKET

Chapter XI

THE CAUSE OF AFRICAN FEVER

Chapter XII

HAUSA WRITINGS AND TRADITIONS

The Hausa Alphabet and Writings—Specimens of Hausa Literature—Examples of the Teaching contained in these Poems;
they represent the best Side of Mohammedan Teaching—
Native Schools throughout Nigeria—Early religious Traditions—Illustrations of Native Reasoning .

Chapter XIII

PROSPECTS OF MOHAMMEDANISM IN AFRICA

Christianity and Islam destined to conquer Africa—Progress of
Islam in the Eastern Sudan; Emin Pasha's Testimony—
Progress in West Africa—The same Religious Toleration
as exists in India will ere long be established—The Good
which Mohammedanism has effected in Africa—Forecast of
its Future suggested by the History of Arabia—Sincerity of
the Prophet's own Religion — Christianity the Interpre-
tation of the Half-truths which he taught .

Chapter XIV

CONCLUSION

Importance of the Anglo-French Treaty of 1898—Sketch of the
Treaty; and of the Anglo-German Agreement of 1899—The
Abolition of Slave-raiding in Nigeria—English Slave-raiders
in West Africa—The Obligation to render the English Protectorate of Nigeria effective—The Gin Question : Action of
the Royal Niger Company in regard to it—The Necessity for
restricting the Trade in Gin and Firearms—The Difficulties
which have yet to be encountered .

Appendices

LIST OF ILLUSTRATIONS

xi

LIST OF ILLUSTRATIONS

ILLUSTRATIONS IN TEXT

MAP

CHAPTER I

INTRODUCTORY

THE British lion is not usually accredited with a tendency to indulge in tears, otherwise we might well conceive of its following the example of Alexander when he realized that the limits of the earth, and therefore of possible conquest, had already been reached. Probably never again will an Englishman open his morning paper to read, as he did on the fifteenth of June 1898, that, by a treaty signed on the previous day, our claim to include within the limits of the British Empire another one per cent. of the population of the globe had been finally accepted by the last of the European Powers that had objected to it. Not one in a thousand of those who glanced at the terms of the treaty, signed after long-protracted negotiations in Paris, would have recognised its immense significance. In the words of a semi-official French newspaper, "To make clear the significance of this arrangement, it is worth while noting that the new frontier just recognised extends over a distance of perhaps not less than 3,000 kilometres (1,875 miles), that is to say, approximately over a space as great as that from Paris to Moscow." The importance of the treaty, however, arises not from the extent of the country to which it relates, nor from the density of its population, but from the exceptional character of its inhabitants.

By the terms of the treaty referred to, the French Government definitely acknowledges our claim to include within our sphere of influence the whole of the territory occupied by the great Hausa-speaking race. The population of the whole district, to which the name Nigeria has recently been given, is probably not less than twenty-five millions, of whom about fifteen millions speak the Hausa language. Apart from our possessions in India and Burmah, there is no native state or combination of states within the limits of the British Empire which can compare in size, population, and importance with this our latest protectorate. Though at the present moment the means of communication between the interior and the coast are of the most primitive kind, the time will come, and that at no distant date, when, by the building of railways and the improvement in other means of transport, the vast populations of the interior will be brought into touch with the coast, and a people two-thirds as numerous as that of Great Britain will afford a new and almost unlimited market for the sale of English goods.

Almost coincident with the signing of the treaty in Paris a discovery is reported to have been made which may yet convert what has been known as "the white man's grave" into something which might even approach a tropical health resort. If it be true, as Dr. Koch suggested several years ago, and as Dr. Ross has apparently demonstrated, that the bacillus of malarial fever is conveyed to man by the bite of a species of mosquito, there ought to be no insuperable difficulty in exterminating this particular species in any neighbourhood inhabited by Europeans. Even where this should prove impossible, the construction of mosquito-proof houses, such as are found in the southern States of America, should minimize the danger of an attack. The two great enemies of the white man in West Africa are fever and dysentery. By adopting the most stringent precautions it is possible for a resident, though perhaps not always for a traveller, to render an attack of the latter unlikely. The former has so far defied all precautions. As far as Europeans are concerned it has placed difficulties in the way of their contracting any other diseases, because it has left them no time in which to be ill of anything else. If, as seems likely, we are about to discover a means of guarding against, possibly too a remedy for, the African malaria, the value of our West African possessions will be enormously enhanced. Hausa-

BOY FROM ASABA, LOWER NIGERIA.

land can never become a British colony in
the same sense as Australia or South Africa,
because, apart from any specific disease, the
climate is so enervating that no white man
would ever care to settle there, still less to
bring his wife and children; but if fever and
dysentery can be successfully combated, he
will be able to settle in it and to exploit its
resources to the same extent as is now possible in India. A resemblance between
Nigeria and India may be pointed out in
respect not only of climate, but of general
culture and civilization. The Hausas, for
example, are no more savages than were the
majority of the peoples of India at the time
when English rule was finally established
amongst them.

The fact that Nigeria lies within the
limits of the Sudan may suggest to some
a possible connection between its inhabitants and the followers of the Mahdi.
Such persons will be surprised to learn that
the Sudan is so large that two individuals
might both be living well within its limits

and yet be five hundred miles further apart than London is from Khartoum. The word Sudan means simply black, and is applied by the natives themselves to practically the whole of Africa north of the Equator and south of the great Sahara, reaching from Senegambia on the west to the Red Sea on the east, its width being thus about four thousand miles. The country to which the name Nigeria has been given, and which is chiefly inhabited by the Hausa people, occupies, as will be seen by reference to the map, about the centre of this vast area. Their country does not come within three hundred miles of the coast at any point, and they are as distinct as possible from the tribes which are found between them and the sea, reaching from Sierra Leone to the mouth of the Congo. These latter are, many of them, the lowest and most degraded savages to be found any- where. In illustration of this statement we may notice the horrible atrocities committed in connection with the fighting which has occurred during the last few years in Dahomey,

Ashanti, Benin, and the hinterland of Sierra Leone. The Hausas are as distinct from these various tribes as is the cultured Bengali from the aboriginal races to be found in some of the mountain districts in India. If the word "civilized" be explained, as it is in Webster's dictionary, as "reclaimed from barbarism," the Hausas have every right to be regarded as a civilized nation. They have developed for themselves, apart from any external assistance, trade and manufactures; they have reduced their language to writing, and have started schools throughout their country for the teaching of their children; and lastly, they have established a more or less stable form of government centralized in a single head. Those who witnessed the march of the Hausa troops in the last Jubilee procession, and who had the opportunity to note their martial bearing and frank, intelligent countenances, will not need to be assured that the men whom they saw wearing the Queen's uniform were worthy to share the honours and to support the traditions of the great British Army.

CHAPTER II

ORIGIN OF THE HAUSA PEOPLE

THE tradition of the Hausas in regard to their early life and habitat, which was reduced to writing in the sixteenth century, and which is universally believed by them, asserts that having originally come from the very far east away beyond Mecca, their ancestors settled first of all in Daura, to the north of Kano. Travelling south from there, they built the town of Kano about 950 years ago, and established the indigo dye works for which Kano is still noted. From Kano and Daura they slowly moved southward, and drove the aboriginal inhabitants from the plains to the mountains. Leaving this tradition for later consideration, let us see what information is available in regard to the early history of the central Sudan as a whole.

HAUSA BOY HOLDING UP CHILD TO ENABLE IT
TO PICK GUAVAS.

In the year which followed the battle of Hastings a Spanish convert to Mohammedanism named el Bikri wrote a book on Africa, parts of which are still extant. His work is of interest, not so much for any fresh information that it contains, but because it enables us to verify several of the dates which are suggested by native tradition. He agrees with the native historian, Ahmed Baba, whose works Dr. Barth saw at Timbuktu, in fixing the conversion to Islam of Za Kasi, king of Songhay, at the beginning of the eleventh century. He tells us that at that date the king of Bornu was still an unbeliever. Native tradition fixes his conversion in 1087. At this time the Hausas must have been a comparatively insignificant people situated between the two great kingdoms of Songhay and Bornu. Songhay was then nearly half the size of Europe, stretching from Sierra Leone to the Middle Niger and beyond, and northwards as far as Morocco. The empire of Bornu was of nearly equal size. In later time, Timbuktu became the most famous city

in the Songhay empire. Both it and the
actual capital, Gogo, are now mere villages.
El Bikri says that the Songhay kings received on their accession to the throne a
sword, a ring, and a copy of the Koran,
which had been brought from Egypt. Towards the end of the sixteenth century the
Sultan of Morocco crossed the desert with an
army of 4,000 men, armed with muskets, and
succeeded in defeating the Songhay army,
which was then unacquainted with the use
of firearms. Then, as the native historian
says, "peaceful repose was succeeded by constant fear; comfort and security by troubles
and suffering; ruin and misfortune took the
place of prosperity; and people began every-
where to fight against each other, so that
property and life became exposed to constant
danger; and this ruin began, spread, increased, and at length prevailed throughout
the whole region." Partly in consequence
of this defeat, and partly owing to the introduction of slave raiding, which dates from
this period, the empire began to decline, and

finally split up into a number of independent states.

Turning from the history of Songhay to that of Bornu, the native tradition, which was probably committed to writing towards the end of the sixteenth century, can be confirmed in several important details by the Arabian historian, Ibn Batuta, who wrote in A.D. 1353. The native chronicles give Ayuma as the name of the first king, his date being A.D. 1000. The first king to embrace Islam was Humé, A.D. 1086. The Hausas in early time evidently regarded the Bornuese people as being closely connected with the Berbers of North Africa, as is shown by their calling a Bornuese man "ba-Berberchi," or the nation "Beriberi." Possibly the connection between the Berbers and the Bornuese ought to be limited to their rulers, as the native chronicle states that up to the beginning of the thirteenth century their kings were of a red complexion like the Arabs. The kingdom of Bornu, as it existed in the Middle Ages, embraced the whole of the provinces now known as Bornu, Kanem, Wadai, Baghirmi, Darfur, and Kordofan. It reached from the Niger to the Nile, a distance of about 1,400 miles. In the thirteenth and again in the sixteenth century it attained a very high degree of civilization and prosperity. In the middle of last century an Arab adventurer seized the throne, soon after which the empire began to break up. It is now confined to the province of Bornu, which is situated on the western shore of Lake Chad, and is about the same size as England. By the recently signed treaty, it is included within the British protectorate. At the present moment the country is ruled, or rather grossly misruled, by an Arab named Rabbah. He was originally a slave of Zubehr Pasha, and afterwards became one of the Mahdi's generals, by whom he was appointed governor of Darfur. Having collected an army in Darfur he threw off his allegiance to the Mahdi, and, marching westwards, subjugated the provinces of Wadai and Darfur. He then attacked the king of Bornu, destroyed his principal town, Kuka,

MASSÛD, FORMERLY A HAUSA SLAVE, THE
AUTHOR'S SERVANT AT TUNIS.

and overran the whole province. At the present time he is in blissful ignorance of the fact that for more than a year past he has been living within the limits of the British Empire.

The history of the two empires, which at one time or another included the greater part of the Hausa country, is much easier to get at than is the history of the Hausa people themselves. The actual word Hausa is not used by Leo Africanus (A.D. 1520), who says that the inhabitants of Zaria, Katsena, and Kano spoke the language of Gober. This can only have been the Hausa language, and it is difficult to explain why he does not actually use the name. According to the mythical genealogy of the Hausas, their original ancestor was Biram, whose grandson Bawu is said to have married a Berber wife, the Hausa race being the offspring of this marriage. This last statement is of extreme interest as suggesting a probable connection between the Hausas and the tribes to the north of the great desert, a connection which is to a cer-

tain extent confirmed by a comparison of the
Hausa and Berber languages. Passing over
the three centuries which followed the sixteenth,
during which very little more is known of the
Hausa people beyond the names of the kings
in their principal cities, we come down to the
year 1802.

A new chapter in the history of the Hausa
people dates from this year. Up to that time,
although most of their rulers had been Mohammedans, the great majority of the Hausas had
remained heathen. Each town had its separate king, most of whom were Hausas, though
in one or two instances the kings were either
Fulahs or members of some other tribe. In
the year 1802, a Fulah sheikh named Othman
dan Fodio began to preach a holy war against
infidels. He suffered many reverses at the
hands of the Hausa kings, but at length succeeded in gathering around him a formidable
army, composed chiefly of Hausas, with which
he established his sway over the whole of the
present Hausa States. On his death in 1817,
the territory which he had conquered was

divided between his brother Abd Allah and
his son Mohammed Bello. The former retained Gando as his capital, and ruled over
the south-western portion of the conquered
territory ; whilst the latter, who was acknowledged as the spiritual head of the whole,
ruled from Sokoto over the remainder, including the important towns of Kano, Katsena,
and Zaria.

This arrangement has lasted down to the
present time. Prior to the time of Othman,
the Fulahs, or, as they are sometimes called,
Fullata, Fulani, or Fulbe, had been settled
in a few scattered communities amongst the
Hausas, and had been chiefly known as pos-
sessors of cattle and as herdsmen. They were
also good horsemen, and were altogether a
much more ambitious and military race than
were the Hausas, to whom trade and commerce
were of almost exclusive interest. The Fulahs
are easily distinguishable in appearance from
the Hausas. Their skin is distinctly lighter,
their nose is better shaped, they are on the
average taller, and they have a keen, cunning

look which is wanting in the frank, open face of the Hausa. They began to settle in Hausa-land about two centuries ago, having migrated from the west, though their own traditions assert that at a still earlier time their ancestors came from the east. What little religious fanaticism exists in Hausaland is confined to the Fulahs, who form the ruling class not only in Sokoto and Gando, but in most of the other Hausa towns.

The form of government now existing in the Hausa country is that of a loose con-federacy of a large number of despotic kings owning a general allegiance either to Gando or Sokoto. This allegiance is shown by the payment of an annual tribute consisting chiefly of slaves ; but it does not in any way prevent the tributary kings from carrying on an almost ceaseless warfare one against another. As long as this tribute, or the greater part of it, continues to be paid in slaves, constant war is a necessity. The marvel is that, despite the fact that every village throughout the country, however small, is a fortified stronghold, and

THREE FULAHS, SHOWING DIFFERENT MODES OF HEAD-DRESS.

that an attack from a slave raider is recognised as an occurrence liable to happen any night in the year, the people have attained to the extraordinary degree of prosperity and civilization which they have. No doubt the African takes life far more philosophically than the European would under similar circumstances. "Sufficient unto the day is the evil thereof" is a principle which characterizes his whole life. In travelling through the country, it was necessary almost every night to keep watch, in view of possible attacks by lions or by hostile natives; but, fully alive as the Hausas professed to be to the danger of attack, they would lie down in front of the fire and go sound asleep, quite careless as to whether we ourselves chose to watch or not. A disposition such as the native possesses is indeed a necessary qualification for living in such a country if life is to be endurable. I remember on one occasion, when travelling with an Armenian companion in Cappadocia; the hut in which we were trying to pass the night having been unsuccessfully attacked by Kurd-

ish brigands, who retired after being fired at,
I asked our host whether the night's experience was an uncommon one. He replied in
the most unconcerned way, No, it happened
on an average about once in twenty days!
This happy indifference to danger, which has
been developed to the utmost in tropical
Africa, certainly tends to decrease the miseries
of existence, if not to actually increase its
pleasures. We shall have something more to
say later on in regard to the havoc wrought
by the slave trade in Hausaland.

To return to the question of the early history of the Hausa people. Apart from any
existing records and from current traditions,
the Hausa language ought to afford us some
clue as to the origin of the people by whom
it is spoken. As has been pointed out, however, in the preface to the Hausa dictionary
which the Cambridge University Press has
recently published, the evidence in regard to
the early habitat of the Hausas is far from
being definite or trustworthy. Nearly a third
of the words in their language are connected

with Semitic roots, most of them having apparently come through the Arabic. On the other hand, two-thirds of the vocabulary bears no resemblance whatever to Arabic. The explanation which would naturally be suggested is that the Semitic roots have been incorporated into the language as the result of intercourse with Arabs who have come across the Sahara Desert. This explanation seems, however, an almost impossible one to adopt when we discover that many of the commonest words, including nearly all the personal pronouns, are of Semitic origin. It has been suggested, and the explanation does not appear altogether impossible, that the presence of a large number of Semitic roots, both in Hausa and in several other West African languages, may be traced back as far as 500 B.C., about which time, according to what is believed to be a Greek translation of an original Carthaginian account, Hanno the Carthaginian set out to endeavour to circumnavigate Africa. His expedition consisted of sixty ships with fifty oars each, containing no less than thirty

thousand men and women, who were intended
to establish a Carthaginian colony at some
point on the coast. The account is of extraordinary interest as being that of the man who
may claim to have been the first explorer of
the dark continent. After rounding Cape
Cantin, they came to a marsh where a number
of elephants were seen disporting themselves.
They passed Cape Verde, the river Gambia,
and the Sierra Leone coast. At the furthest
point they reached they saw "wild men and
women covered with hair." Hanno's interpreter called these creatures "gorilla," and
three of their skins, which he brought back to
Carthage with him, were afterwards hung up
in the temple of Kronos. The ape which we
now know as the gorilla was so called because
it was supposed, when first seen, to be identical
with the creature which Hanno saw. Assuming the identification to be correct, it would be
an almost certain proof that Hanno's expedition
reached as far as the Congo. On the other
hand, it is at least possible that the gorilla so
named by Hanno's interpreter is to be identi-

fied with the chimpanzee which is still to be found on the Sierra Leone coast. The language which Hanno's colonists spoke would have been Semitic, and, assuming them to have survived the many dangers that would have beset them, alike from the hostility of the natives and the unhealthiness of the climate, it is just conceivable that they may have introduced the Semitic element, which is common to many of the languages on the coast and in the interior.

An attempt to reach Nigeria from the north was made by a Roman general named Septimus Flaccus, who is said to have set out from Fezzan at about the time of the Christian era, and, after marching across the desert for three months, to have reached "the black man's country." A few years later another Roman, Julius Maternus, starting from southern Fezzan, and crossing the desert, reached Agisymba, which is probably to be identified with Bornu or Kanem. His march occupied four months, and he speaks of the country as abounding in rhinoceroses, a statement which

is applicable to this country to-day. Neither
of these last expeditions, unfortunately, throw
any light upon the inhabitants of the country
or the language which they spoke.

The Hausas assert that their ancestors came
from the very far east away beyond Mecca.
In support of this statement, it may be pointed
out that a slight resemblance may be traced
between the Hausa and Berber languages, and
again between the Berber and Coptic. The
resemblance, however, is rather in the construction of the languages than in their actual
vocabulary, and is not sufficient to establish
any certain connection. If it should prove
possible to do so, and the Hausa tradition as
to the origin of their race could be accepted
as trustworthy, the Hausa, Berber, and Coptic
languages would carry us back to a time before
the Semites entered Africa ; that is, probably
about 2,500 B.C., when an earlier stream of
immigrants, coming from the same direction,
and speaking a language akin to their suc-
cessors, spread over the north, and eventually
over the interior of the continent. What will

appear to many the insuperable difficulty connected with such a theory is, that whereas
many of the Berbers and Copts are as light-
coloured as the inhabitants of Southern Europe,
the Hausas are as black as any people in the
world. It seems very hard to believe that
such a change could have occurred within
many thousands of years; and if any certain
connection between the Hausa and Berber
languages be established, we should probably
be compelled to assume that the Hausa language was introduced from the north, and was
imposed upon them by some unknown race
who conquered them in very early time, and
of whom all tradition has now been lost. If,
as Darwin suggested, the human race originated in or near Somaliland, it would seem
natural to suppose that the negroes and the
Hausas, Fulahs and other races to whom the
term negro cannot strictly be applied, have
never left Africa, but have gradually spread
from east to west. In this case the Semites
must have migrated eastward before the dawn
of history, crossing into Asia probably by way

of the Straits of Bab-el-Mandeb. A small section of them returning to Africa by way of Egypt in very much later time must then be assumed to have influenced to a very considerable and permanent extent the languages of the interior. An immense amount of careful study, not simply of Hausa, but of all the surrounding languages, will be required before it will be possible to speak with any certainty as to the origin of the Hausa language or people. Nowhere is there so wide and inviting a field for students of languages as that afforded in the interior of West Africa. The language spoken, for example, by perhaps eight or ten million people in Bornu is unknown to a single scholar in Europe, though a few materials were collected for its study by Dr. Barth half a century ago. It is earnestly to be hoped that a serious attempt will be made to study this and several other neighbouring languages, which would probably well repay the time spent upon them.

HAUSA SOLDIERS OF THE R.N. CO.'S FORCE, INCLUDING TWO NON-COMMISSIONED OFFICERS.

CHAPTER III

THE HAUSA SOLDIER

TO the majority of English people the word Hausa was unknown until our first war against Ashanti, in 1874. A small body of Hausa troops took part in that expedition, and, according to the testimony of its leader, the present Commander-in-Chief, afforded invaluable aid to the British troops. During the next twenty years they were employed in gradually increasing numbers as police in all the British possessions on the West Coast. In the last Ashanti war, in 1895, they formed a considerable proportion of the whole number of troops engaged. They have been employed as police and as soldiers by the Royal Niger Company ever since its formation ; indeed, the work of the Company could not have been carried on without their aid.

Lastly, the British public had the opportunity of witnessing the march past during the Jubilee procession of three detachments of Hausas, numbering forty-two in all, who had been brought over to England for the occasion. Our neighbours across the water have shown their appreciation of the soldierly qualities possessed by the Hausas, and have sent a detachment of Hausa troops, recruited in Dahomey, to serve in Madagascar.

It might naturally, then, be supposed that the Hausa was a born soldier, and that the European governments by giving him the opportunity to enlist had only afforded the means for gratifying his instinctive love of fighting. So far, however, is this from being the case that the Hausas are one of the least warlike races to be found in West Africa. As has already been pointed out, they have allowed themselves to be conquered, and have remained for nearly a century in subjection to a race which they themselves outnumbered by ten to one. The Hausa is by natural instinct not a soldier, but a trader, and it is his love of trade which first brought him down to the coast, and so into touch with the English recruiting officer.

The question then suggests itself, how is it that a race of traders should become such splendid soldiers as the Hausas have proved themselves to be? The answer no doubt is that the superiority which the Hausa undoubtedly possesses arises not from any natural aptness for fighting, but from a superiority of character. This superiority is especially noticeable when Hausas are employed as police, as they are, for instance, in Lagos. A native policeman belonging to any other tribe is always open to receive a bribe, and cannot be depended on to act in any emergency or to arrest any one whom he regards as his superior. A Hausa policeman, on the other hand, is almost as incorruptible as an English judge, and loves to show his own importance by arresting any one who furnishes him with a sufficient excuse. It is this force of character, combined with a physical strength which is, I believe, unsurpassed by any people in the world, that makes the Hausa the efficient soldier he is. Whilst I was watching some of the Hausa troops in the employ of the Royal Niger Company at Lokoja, the English officer in command pointed to a small mountain gun on the ground, and asked if I could lift it. With extreme difficulty I succeeded in raising it an inch from the ground. He then told me that one of their Hausa soldiers had the duty assigned him of carrying this gun on his head whenever the troops were on the march. On my expressing my incredulity, the officer sent for the Hausa, and ordered him to put the gun up on his head and march across the ground, an order which he obeyed with alacrity. The officer further informed me that on one occasion when they had been compelled to make a forced march through the forest land near the river, this man carried the gun for twenty-two miles in the course of the day. My own experience when marching in the interior was that a Hausa would carry without grumbling nearly twice as much as the carriers recruited from any other tribe.

The Hausas are quite amenable to discipline, but in actual fighting their fearless impetuosity, combined with their love of looting, makes them at times very difficult to restrain.

The British Empire includes so many districts, we might almost say countries, inhabited by turbulent and half-civilized peoples, that seldom a week passes without soldiers being called into requisition in order to put down some disturbance or repel some raid. In India we are fortunate enough to include amongst our subjects some of the best fighting material to be found anywhere. In view of the enormous expansion of our empire in the continent of Africa, it may well afford ground for congratulation that our latest Protectorate can supply us with as many soldiers as we can ever have occasion to employ—soldiers, too, whose fellow-countrymen have stood side by side with our English troops in many a hard-fought fight.

It might, perhaps, be suggested that the Hausa could not be safely relied upon in fighting against those of his own race and his own religion. Patriotism, however, in our English sense of the word, is a virtue unknown in West Africa. Slave raiding, and the existence of innumerable petty kings, combine to prevent the average Hausa from possessing any great affection for his country considered as a whole. The latter difficulty—namely, that of leading Mohammedans to fight against Mohammedans —is a much more real one, but, as the recent campaign against Bida has shown, it is by no means insuperable.

A short notice of the campaign, which resulted in the capture of Bida in January, 1897, will illustrate the fighting qualities possessed by the Hausas. Bida is a town containing a population of about sixty thousand, most of whom are Nupés, though the ruling caste are Fulahs, as is the case throughout the Hausa States. It is situated about twenty-five miles from the left bank of the Niger, four hundred miles up from the sea. On approaching the town in 1895, I had the misfortune to be mistaken for a Frenchman, and a sudden attack which was made on my party very nearly brought our expedition to an untimely end. As it was, we were detained by the king as his prisoners for a week, until he had received convincing proofs as to our nationality. At this time a treaty existed between the king and the Royal Niger Company, by which he bound himself not to interfere with traders passing through his territory, and not to make slave raids on the southern bank of the river Niger. As illustrating the depopulating character of these raids, it may be mentioned that in the course of a very few years one of the tribes on the southern bank of the river was reduced from sixty thousand to five thousand. Owing to his persistent disregard of this treaty, and the wholesale raids which he continued to make, the Company decided to send an expedition to attack him. The king of Bida, towards the end of 1896, had sent his chief general, called the Markum, across the Niger, partly in order to raid for slaves and partly in order to threaten the Company's station at Lokoja, a town at the junction of the rivers Niger and Binué. Sir

George Goldie, the Governor of the Royal Niger Company, accompanied by twenty-five English officers and five hundred Hausa troops, left Lokoja on the 6th of January, and advanced to meet the Fulah and Nupé troops under the command of the Markum. Seldom, if ever, was an expedition organized in which forethought and courage were so combined, and in which so little margin was allowed for the possibility of a mistake. Five hundred Hausas were being led for the first time to attack their co-religionists, who outnumbered them, as it eventually proved, by fifty to one. Their opponents were for the most part expert horsemen, armed with guns and spears. If we compare the force sent at about the same time by the English Government against the king of Benin, who had not a quarter as many troops as the king of Bida, we shall be in a position to appreciate the courage and skill of those who planned and carried through the Bida campaign. The number of troops employed against Benin were four times as numerous as those employed against Bida, and

HAUSA MALLAM AND SOLDIER.

[The Mallam acts as Mohammedan chaplain to the Hausa troops.]

nearly half of these were Englishmen. No doubt a Company can afford to run somewhat greater risks than a Government, but it must have required no small amount of courage to accept the responsibility for an expedition in which a comparatively slight miscalculation or blunder would have involved the annihilation of the whole force.

Every care was taken to soothe the religious susceptibilities of the Hausas, who were all Mohammedans. Two " mallams " were engaged to act as chaplains to the force, and prayers were said by them in camp three times a day. With the troops marched 900 carriers. No fighting took place on the southern bank of the river, as the Markum's army dispersed on the approach of the Hausa force. The force which crossed the Niger to march on Bida consisted of 32 Europeans, 507 native soldiers, and 565 carriers. On the 26th of January, three days after the crossing of the river, the little force drew near to Bida without having encountered any serious opposition. A reconnaissance as far as the ridge overlooking

Bida, and distant from the walls a little more than a mile, was now made by rather less than half the force, the rest being left in charge of the baggage and the guns. On the arrival of the former division on the ridge, a countless multitude both of horsemen and infantry were observed moving to and fro beneath the walls of the city. A few shots having been fired, the reconnoitring party was ordered to retire in order to rejoin their comrades in charge of the camp, which was nearly two miles to the rear. The really critical moment of the campaign now arrived. The withdrawal of the reconnoitring party was interpreted by the Nupés as a confession of failure. A great shout arose from those in front of the walls, followed by a rapid concentration of a large body of horsemen, who charged up the hill, and soon succeeded in surrounding the retreating square.

The number of the enemy was perhaps twenty thousand, the number of Hausas and English rather more than two hundred. The Maxim guns placed at the corners of the

square were served by the English officers.
As the amount of ammunition was limited, the
Hausas were ordered to wait until the enemy
came within about two or three hundred yards
and then fire volleys. Again and again the
horsemen charged, some using guns, others with
spear or sword brandished aloft. It was
obvious that if they could but once touch the
firing line, and a hand-to-hand fight were to
ensue, they would be instantly victorious. But,
though on one occasion they got within about
twenty yards of the square, the steady volleys
of the Hausas drove them back with their
ranks decimated many times over. The
Hausas, so far from showing the least sign of
fear, laughed and jeered at them and called to
them to come on. Had they wavered for a
moment, or the slightest panic occurred, no one
would have survived to tell the tale. As it
was, they moved steadily back in unbroken
formation till, to the immense relief of the
officers in command, they came in sight of the
camp, and received the support of the fire from
the troops which had been left to guard it.

Soon after sunset the same evening the twelve-pounder gun which had been dragged all day long with the utmost difficulty over ploughed fields, small watercourses, fallen trees, etc., arrived in camp. Some one suggested that a shot should be fired in the direction of Bida, which was more than three miles distant, and separated from the camp by a ridge of hills. The gun was accordingly fired at 8 p.m. It was aimed with the aid of a compass, and was sighted to its highest range—viz., 5,400 yards. Three days later it was ascertained that the shell which was fired burst close beside the Markum's palace in Bida. A second shell, fired three hours later, burst just outside the king's palace. It is hard to realize in any degree the horror and amazement which the sudden appearance of these death-dealing portents in the dead of night must have caused to men accustomed to nothing more formidable than the ordinary rifle.

Though to some extent disheartened by the terrible loss which they had suffered on the previous day, the Nupés were still confident

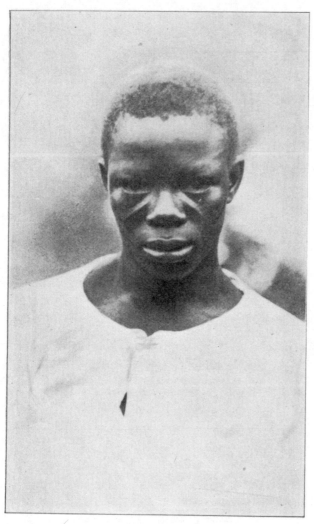

NUPÈ BOY, SHOWING TRIBAL MARKS.

that their overwhelming numbers would in the long run secure to them the victory. As the Hausas began to move forward in square formation, with the carriers in the centre, the experience of the previous day was repeated. The enemy surrounded them in countless numbers, and attempted again and again to charge. The square, however, moved steadily forward till it reached the slope of a hill about a quarter of a mile from the wall. The big gun was now brought into requisition, and shells were dropped at different places all over the town, destroying and setting fire to many of the houses. Incendiary rockets were also used with great effect. About noon it became apparent that the enemy were convinced of the impossibility of offering further resistance, and that they had begun to leave the town. The same afternoon the Hausa troops entered through a breach which had been made in the walls, and on the 29th Sir George Goldie and the whole of the little force entered and occupied the king's palace. The casualties were almost incredibly small, considering the desperate character of the fighting which had taken place. They were one English officer and seven men killed and nine men wounded.

Thus ended the most important battle ever fought in West Africa. Its importance is derived not only from the fact that it was the first real blow struck at the slave raiding of the interior, but, perhaps still more, from the proof which it afforded of the fighting powers possessed by our Hausa levies in West Africa. A treaty was concluded by which the Markum was recognised as king in place of the former king, Abu Bekri, who had fled, the southern part of the Nupé country, which had been depopulated by slave raiding, was ceded to the Company, and the Company's protectorate over the northern portion, including Bida, was definitely acknowledged. Immediately after the signing of this treaty the Hausa troops were pushed forward to attack the king of Ilorin, who had for some time past been indulging in hostile demonstrations against the people of Ibadan, at the back of the Lagos colony, who were under our protection. As the Hausa force was approaching Ilorin, the enemy suddenly appeared, but fortunately they had just time in which to form a square, before the attack was delivered. The result was the same as it had been outside Bida : the enemy's horsemen charged with reckless courage, but were met with volleys delivered by the Hausas, who were if possible still more confident and determined than they had been in the former fights. The Fulahs and Yorubas, of whom the king's army was composed, fell back at length, after suffering severe loss. The fight was renewed on the following day, and it was not till the town had been bombarded and set on fire in several places that the people recognised the uselessness of further resistance. A treaty was eventually signed with the king, by which he agreed to abstain from making war and to place his territory under the protection of the Company. This latter treaty has been observed by the natives, and a large amount of trade with Ilorin is now going on. That with Bida was broken almost as soon as it was made, as the king, who had fled, and by the terms of the treaty had been desposed, returned after the departure of the Hausa troops, and was reinstated by the people in his former position. His return meant the revival of slavery and the slave trade in and around Bida, and the renewal of restrictions which had been placed upon legitimate trade. Although one of the objects with which the expedition was conducted has thus failed of immediate accomplishment, the expedition was in the most real sense a success. It demonstrated the possibility of attacking the slave raiders of the central Sudan with soldiers recruited from their own subjects, it set free many hundreds of slaves, and it abolished both slave raiding and slavery permanently over a large area on the southern bank of the river Niger. A further outcome of the expedition was that on Jubilee Day the status of slavery was declared to be abolished on the whole of the river Niger within the Company's jurisdiction, and an invitation was given to any, whether slaves or free, to settle in the Kabba district, on the southern bank of the Niger, the settlers being

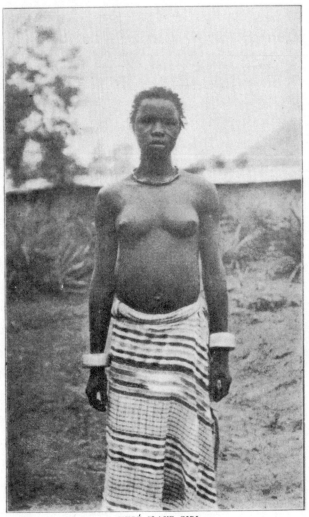

A NUPÉ SLAVE GIRL.

[The armlets are made of natron.]

guaranteed the protection of the English flag. The large body of slaves who followed the expedition on its return from Bida have since been settled in a tract of country a few miles below Lokoja, to which the name Victoria has been appropriately given.

As the Hausa expedition was returning down the river after capturing Ilorin, the news of the Benin massacre, which had occurred about two months before, was received. Sir George Goldie at once telegraphed to England offering to the Government the services of the Hausa troops for an expedition against Benin. Arrangements had, however, already been completed, and the Hausa lost the opportunity of adding another victory to their already distinguished record.

CHAPTER IV

AMONGST THE HAUSAS

THE Hausas are, as a general rule, extremely hospitable to strangers. Though their babies scream with horror at the sight of a white man, and the odour which his skin emits is to them peculiarly disagreeable, they are nearly always ready to welcome and entertain the stranger. It is true that the word to talk is indistinguishable in sound in their language from the word to fight, but their vocabulary was, no doubt, the outcome of their intercourse one with another rather than with foreigners, so that the similarity of sound is not as ominously suggestive to the outsider as might at first appear. Politeness is such a marked characteristic of the Hausas that a stranger could almost distinguish them from other natives by a careful observation of their

demeanour. A Hausa will very seldom pass
one of his fellow-countrymen, much less a
stranger, without saluting him. Should the
greeting be returned, he will very likely inter-
rupt his journey and pause for several minutes
to pour forth a series of salutations adapted to
the circumstances of the case. Under the
word "sanu" in the Hausa dictionary will be
found specialized forms, such as, Greetings to
your weariness! *i.e.*, May you not be overtired,
Greetings to you amidst the rain; Greetings to
you in your loneliness, an expression often
used on the death of a friend; May you be
happy over your work, etc.

The Hausas are of medium height; their
lips project slightly and are thicker than those
of a European, but not so thick as in the case
of a typical negro. Their skin is perfectly
black; they are accustomed to keep their faces
and heads clean shaven, the operation of
shaving being performed with a razor of native
manufacture, the iron for which is obtained and
smelted in their own country. Soap is not, as
a rule, used in connection with the operation.

The illustration shows a Hausa iron razor, together with the leather case in which it is usually kept. Both men and women, especially the latter, paint their eyelids and eyebrows with *antimony powder*. The powder is of a leaden,

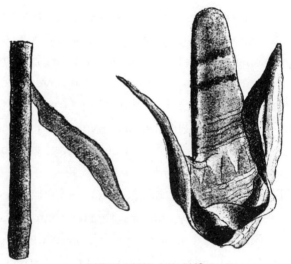

NATIVE RAZOR AND CASE.

grey colour, and produces a sort of iridescent, metallic lustre. The use which the Hausas make of it is one of extreme antiquity. The statement in 2 Kings ix. 30 regarding Jezebel, "she painted her eyes," is translated by

Jerome, who was well acquainted with the
customs of the East : " she put antimony powder (stibium) upon her eyes." The illustration,
which is half the natural size, shows the little

CASE MADE OF SKIN, FOR HOLDING ANTIMONY POWDER.

skin box in which antimony powder is carried.
The cover pulls off. The custom may either
have been introduced into Nigeria by Arabs or,
as seems equally probable, may have originated
afresh amongst the Hausas.

Every Hausa, old or young, heathen or Mohammedan, carries one or more *charms* on his person. Many of them carry quite a large collection of such. One or two of my porters, in addition to carrying a double load weighing a hundred-weight and a half, carried charms weighing several additional pounds. Every native who has been on the pilgrimage to Mecca is believed to have acquired the power of writing charms. Some of them are short extracts from the Koran, others consist of apparently meaningless symbols, others of a piece of wood or hair. In nearly every case the charm is wrapped in a piece of leather. The charms are believed to have the power of warding off disease, of securing victory in battle, of causing one's enemy to die, of procuring riches and happiness, and of effecting, in fact, almost anything that the wearer may desire. Some charms are not intended to be worn, but are written out on a flat piece of wood, which serves the purpose of a slate ; the ink is then washed off and drunk by the person who wishes to benefit by the charm. The one

HAUSA CHARM

of which an illustration is here given is intended to be treated in this way. Unless the information which was given to me in regard to this particular charm be incorrect, any person whom the drinker of the mixture is thinking of at the time when he drinks will forthwith conceive an affection for him. On two occasions I was applied to and asked to provide charms : on the first the applicant desired one that would not merely prevent bullets striking him in battle, but turn them back on his foes; on the other occasion I was desired to provide a charm or medicine which should cause a runaway wife to return to the person who was to drink it. The belief in the efficacy of charms is common to the Mohammedans, the pagans, and probably to most of the native Christians in West Africa.

Drums of various shapes and sizes are extremely common amongst the Hausas. They are usually made out of a wooden cylinder formed by scooping out the trunk of a tree, and stretching a goat's skin over one or both ends. The drum plays a most important part, not only in state processions and war, but in the conduct of every-day business. The quickest way a native has of transmitting news in Africa is by means of his drum. When, as is often the case, villagers are sufficiently near to allow the drum in one village to be heard in the next, messages of some considerable length can be passed over wide districts far more quickly than by any known means other than the electric wire. In the case of a European traveller, the impression which he has produced in the first village is often transmitted to the second. A few beats on the drum will explain to the people to whom he is coming whether he is to be received as a friend or as an enemy, whether his party is large or small, and similar details of interest. Should no message have been sent in advance, the drummer on the outskirts of the village which he is entering will announce his opinions in regard to the stranger to his fellow-villagers by beating on the drum. Again and again, as I have entered a village in Central Africa, I have heard the drum proclaiming aloud the

NATIVE DRUMS.

sort of person I was supposed to be, and have vainly wished to be able to interpret its beats. On one occasion, when spending the night in the camp of a slave raider, whose intentions appeared to be the reverse of satisfactory, a drummer stationed himself outside my tent, and commenced to beat with what appeared to be ominous vigour, though, as the event proved, without any evil intent.

The art of *poisoning* is developed amongst the Hausas, though by no means to the same extent that it is amongst the tribes on the river Niger. Amongst the latter, poison is probably responsible for as many deaths as all diseases put together. It is regarded as such a natural and obvious thing to poison any one whose presence has for any reason become objection-able that even natives professing Christianity find it hard to be asked to abandon the custom. A native minister of some standing on the river Niger thought it necessary to assure his white guest, in regard to one dish after another which he offered him, that this particular dish did not contain any poison. The chief use

which the Hausas make of poison is to place
it on their arrows. They use for this purpose
both vegetable poisons and poison obtained
from the dead body of an enemy, though the
latter use would probably be confined to the
pagan Hausas.

The *houses*[1] in which the Hausas live, including even the palaces of kings, are built of mud.
This must not be taken as suggesting that the
houses are mere hovels, or that many of them
are not fine and imposing buildings. Timber
cannot be used in Hausaland, owing to the
depredations of the white ants, and it would
not be easy to build a house of any size with
stone if no other material could be used at the
same time. In the case of the smaller houses,
the roof is constructed of reeds resembling
bamboos in appearance, as the white ants do
not regard these as edible. The roofs of the
larger houses are made in the shape of a dome,
and are made with hardened mud. The mud,
both of the walls and roofs, is often smoothed
and marked so as to resemble stone, and is

[1] See illustrations pp. 70, 73.

occasionally covered with coloured decoration.
Except in Kano, where the custom has been
introduced by Arabs from the north, houses
with two storeys are unknown. The Hausa
word for house includes the courtyard and the
separate rooms which the courtyard contains.
Owing to the fact that building is almost entirely of mud, and that towns and villages are
constantly being obliterated by slave-raiders,
no buildings of any antiquity are to be found
in the country. The walls by which the larger
cities are surrounded are built with great care,
and, from a defensive point of view, are quite
as strong as if they were made of stone.

The Hausa *dress* attracts the attention of
the traveller, alike from the excellence of the
material of which it is made and the fact that it
is so extremely becoming. The cloth is for
the most part produced in and around Kano.
It is made of native - grown cotton, and is
usually dyed either blue or scarlet. It is woven
on looms never more than four inches wide,
but the strips are so neatly sewn together that
except by close examination the joins would

not be detected. A large amount of English cloth is now imported by way of the Niger, and in view of the conservative habits of the Hausa people the cloth introduced is an imitation, both as regards pattern and colour, of their own. I was shown some time ago in England a large piece of blue cloth, which was regarded by its owner as a most valuable specimen of native Hausa work, but a close examination proved that it had been woven on a very wide loom, and that its birthplace was not Kano, but Manchester. It had, no doubt, been out to West Africa, and had been re-imported as a curiosity. The ordinary dress is in the form of a loose surplice with wide flaps covering the arms. It has also a pocket in front of immense size, which is used as a convenient receptacle for the owner's possessions, or would-be possessions. Honesty, in the particular sense in which we use the word, is not an universal virtue amongst the Hausas. If a Hausa comes to pay a call and your attention should be distracted for a moment, he has an uncomfortable habit of sweeping up any

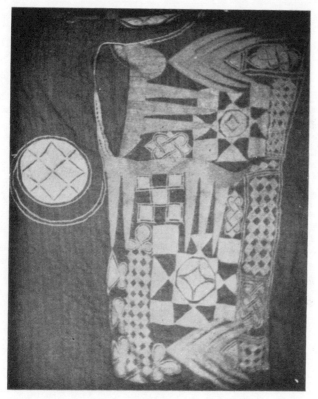

HAUSA TOBE.   THE PATTERN EMBROIDERED ON THE POCKET
IS UNIFORM THROUGHOUT THE COUNTRY.

superfluous articles he may happen to catch sight of and carrying them off in the folds of his capacious pocket. A friend of mine had no less bulky an article than a cornet carried away in this fashion. The politeness of the Hausa visitor, which it is impossible not to reciprocate, renders it also impossible to make any inquiries as to the articles which have disappeared. The outside dress or tobe is often beautifully embroidered with needlework. The pattern, as represented in the illustration, is very elaborate, and is uniform throughout the whole country. In addition to a tobe, the Hausas wear very loose baggy trousers somewhat in the style of the Arabs, also a kind of shirt made of the same material as the tobe. The women[1] wear a rather plainer and more tightly fitting tobe than the men. Boots and shoes are not, as a rule, worn when on the march, but are carried and put on on reaching a town. The Hausas, like the Israelites of old, make large use of "rams' skins dyed red." From these are made sandals, riding boots,

[1] See illustration p. 184.

mats, pillows and many different articles, some
of which are very pretty and artistic. They
export considerable quantities of these skins
to America *viâ* Tripoli, the leather being so
well prepared that it is of considerable com-

HAUSA HAT WORN BY THE AUTHOR.

mercial value. The only other article of
Hausa dress is the cap or hat. The typical
Hausa hat (see illustration) is made of plaited
grass ornamented with red leather. It is of
immense size, the one I wore being nineteen

inches across, or four and a half feet in cir-
cumference. It serves the double purpose of
an umbrella and a sunshade, and is greatly
superior to a pith helmet or any other hat that
I know. Many of the Hausas wear inside
a small cloth cap or a fez. As far as protection against the sun is concerned, they do not
appear to need any covering for their heads.
I have frequently seen Hausas with shaven
heads lolling about under a tropical mid-day
sun, the thermometer standing perhaps at 160°.
Were an Englishman to do the same for five
seconds, the experiment would probably be a
fatal one. Either the native skull is more
impervious than that of the European, or, by
a process of the survival of the fittest, all those
capable of suffering from sunstroke have long
ago perished.

Rings made of brass, wood inlaid with
ornamental brass work, or of natron, are very
commonly worn, especially by the women.
They are one or two inches in width, and are
worn on the wrists or ankles.[1] They are sel-

[1] See illustrations pp. 40, 190.

dom taken off, being often so tight as to make their removal a matter of serious difficulty, and are washed and polished on the wearer.

Baskets of different shapes, many of them worked in most elegant patterns, are made of grass. Mats, fans, dishes and vases are made of the same material. The art of pottery is developed to a considerable extent. For small water jugs the gourd shown in the illustration is used. It is much lighter than one made of pottery, and is quite strong enough for its purpose. Variegated patterns are frequently cut into the outside of the gourd. The basket in the illustration is covered with cowrie shells. It was made in Bornu and carried across the Sahara to Tripoli by a native caravan.

The *bedsteads* in a Hausa house are made of reeds. They raise the occupant about eighteen inches from the ground, and are used during the daytime as seats or couches. In some instances the bedstead is constructed of mud hardened like the walls of the house. Underneath is a hollow place, in which it is

WATER-JUG AND BASKET.   THE JUG IS A GOURD WHICH HAS
BEEN SCOOPED OUT AND IS USED FOR CARRYING WATER.
THE BASKET IS COVERED WITH COWRY SHELLS.

customary to light a fire. As I found once by experience, these bedsteads are not always built as strongly as desirable, and are apt to let the sleeper descend into the fireplace in the midst of his slumbers. Should the fire happen to be still alight, the consequences are apt to be of a serious nature.

Infants are always carried by their mothers on their backs, a long roll of cloth which is wound tightly round mother and child serving to keep it in position. Women will often travel long distances and do their ordinary day's work with their infants behind them. A woman whom I engaged at Kano to grind wheat and to act as a sort of charwoman carried out her work, which often involved a good deal of stooping, with her child tightly affixed to her. The children of Hausas, like those of other native races, are at birth of a dirty yellowish brown colour, a fact which seems strongly to suggest that this was the colour of the Central African races in a past by no means inconceivably distant. For the first few years the Hausa children are distinctly serious, if not mournful, but by the time they have reached the age of six or seven they are as merry and full of fun as could be

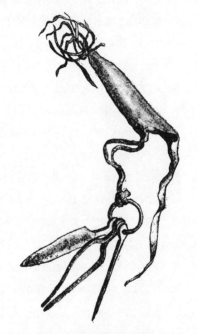

INSTRUMENT FOR EXTRACTING CORNS.

desired.   Cheerfulness is one of the most marked characteristics, not only of Hausa children, when once they have passed the earliest stage, but of the men and women.

BEDOUIN WOMAN WITH CHILD.

However wet, uncomfortable, and tired our carriers were after a long day's march, once the fire was lit and they had provided themselves with something to eat, they soon became as merry as possible.

The illustration represents the surgical instruments which a Hausa doctor makes use of for the purpose of extracting corns. They are made of native iron and enclosed in the little leather case to which they are fastened. The characteristic feature of native surgery is its heroic character. The accepted cure for indigestion or stomach ache is to lay the patient down on the ground and for the doctor and perhaps one or more assistants to jump on the part from which the pain proceeds.

CHAPTER V

THE DAY'S MARCH

PERHAPS the easiest way in which to enable the reader to realize what a day's march is like is to give, in diary form, the experience of a specimen day. In the following sketch everything happened exactly as described, though the incidents did not quite all of them occur on the same day.

Soon after midnight I was awaked by our Arab servant, who came to say that a lion or some animal of similar appearance was about to attack us. If the fear depicted on my servant's face had been any guarantee for the truth of his statement, I should have thought it necessary to prepare a suitable reception for the lion, but having learnt by experience that it was undesirable to pay too much attention to his reports, I turned over and endeavoured to get to sleep. Success having just crowned my efforts, I was again awaked by a sudden blow on the forehead. It was not, however, the lion's paw, but the body of a lizard which met my grasp on putting my hand up in the dark to discover what had happened. The reptile in question had been sleeping, after the manner of his class, with his feet clinging to the roof of my hut and his body parallel with the ground. Disturbed by some ill dream, or having fallen perhaps into more than usually profound slumber, he had relaxed his hold, the final result being as above described. I had but just got to sleep for the second time when a slight movement on the part of one of my companions caused me to look up, and I saw, standing in the hole that served instead of a doorway, an unusually fine hyæna, with its eyes fixed steadily upon us. As it was lighter outside than in, we could see the hyæna much more distinctly than it could see us. My companion, Dr. Tonkin, was in the act of hurling a heavy boot at our visitor just as I awoke. The boot hit the hyæna full in the face, and caused the immediate abandonment of any hostile intentions which it may have been harbouring against us. The next time that I managed to fall asleep I was left undisturbed for upwards of an hour. The cause of my awaking this time was no blow or even sound, but a rapidly increasing sense of extreme discomfort. Hitherto the disturbers of our slumber had arrived singly; on this occasion their number was equal to the population of one of the largest of our English towns. We were invaded by an army of the much-dreaded travelling ants. I had seen these ants crossing our line of march on one or two occasions, but they had not deigned to take any notice of our presence. Now, however, they had arrived bent on nothing short of murder; and had we not decided that prudence was better than valour, and beat a rapid retreat, there is good reason to suppose that they would have accomplished their object. As it was, by our abandoning our hut and ignominiously running away the ants had to content themselves with eating the lizards,

cockroaches, beetles, and other ants which had
shared the hut with us, but had not been
sufficiently agile to effect their escape. The
rest of the night was spent by us in a
state of disconsolate misery, crouching in the
corner of another hut at a respectful distance
from our own. On returning a little before sun-
rise we found no trace whatever of our disturbers, who, after eating everything living in our
hut had no doubt gone on to pay some other
call. We then proceeded to rouse our carriers,
who had been sleeping out of range of the
travelling ants, and to make ready for the
day's march. The fire having been lighted,
our cook got ready the breakfast, which consisted of some native cakes of guinea corn
and rice, together with some tea. The latter
was made with water which was the colour
of tea before being put on the fire, with two
or three of Burroughs & Wellcome's tea
tabloids added, in order to make the taste
correspond with the colour. Breakfast ended,
I picked up one of my boots, which had been
left lying on the ground, and found inside a

small colony of white ants, who were busily engaged in devouring the sole. On tipping them out on the ground a number of ants that had till then kept themselves out of sight ran towards the spot, and seizing a white ant apiece in their mouths, ran off with them. Whether the white ants were intended for food or for use as slaves, as is the custom with some of the African ants, I was unable to ascertain. The other boot, which had got very wet on the previous day, had been left out in the sun after our arrival, the result being that one whole side of the boot had split in such a way as to render it perfectly useless. As I was engaged in hunting up another pair, our head-carrier came to say that he was informed that the district into which we were about to march was inhabited by cannibals, and that he and his companions were reluctant to run the risk of being eaten. I expressed my utmost sympathy, assuring him at the same time that the last thing I should think of doing would be to furnish food for a cannibal repast, and that I was prepared to personally guarantee the safety of all my companions. After some further discussion the man appeared to be satisfied, and went away to complete the preparations for starting. Presently I heard a loud noise outside, accompanied by shouts and scuffling, and going out, found that my carriers had fallen to fighting amongst themselves. The crisis was reached when one of them picked up a stick, six feet or so in length, and brandishing it aloft, brought it down with a resounding crash on the bald head of his neighbour. The blow would have stunned, if it had not killed, any ordinary individual, but in this case the recipient merely rubbed his hand across his head, at the same time expressing his acquiescence in the sentiments with which the blow had been accompanied. The fight ended, two or three of the carriers came up to me to say that one of their companions had over-exerted himself on the previous day's march, and required a rest of at least a day before proceeding any further. They hoped that I would agree that it would be best for him and for them to stay where they were till the porter in question had recovered. I expressed in some of the most forcible words which the Hausa language contains my entire disapproval of their proposal and my incredulity as to the reported indisposition of the carrier. They smiled and said that perhaps I was right, and that they would prepare to start immediately. However, on going amongst them some twenty minutes later, I found that they had altered their mind, and that several small groups of them were engaged in a gambling game played with cowrie shells. Meanwhile the sun was steadily rising and the best part of the day for purposes of marching had already passed. After half an hour's further discussion, some three hours having now elapsed since we had our breakfast, I collected all the carriers who could be spared from the gambling and resolved to push on ahead, in the hope that when the rest discovered that their companions had actually started they would be willing to follow with the remainder of the luggage, which I had left under the charge of Dr. Tonkin. Happily this surmise proved to be correct,

and before midday we had reunited our party
and were well under weigh. Our carriers, who
numbered sixty altogether, had the disagreeable
habit of straggling one behind the other, till
our procession became sometimes a mile in
length. As we were marching through forest
land, with deep, intersecting gullies and occasional patches of open country covered with
grass ten or twelve feet in height, this habit
became not only disagreeable, but a source of
positive danger. The district through which we
were marching was known to be infested by
brigands and slave-raiders, and nothing could
have suited their purpose better, had they
thought fit to attack us, than the straggling
nature of our procession. We had arranged
that the repeated firing of a rifle at any
point in our line should be regarded by
the rest of our party as a sign that an attack was expected, or was being delivered at
that particular point. As I was marching at
the head of our procession I heard the un-
welcome signal some distance to the rear.
Hastening back to ascertain the cause, I dis-

covered that the firing had been intended to signify that Dr. Tonkin and the last batch of porters had taken a wrong turning and had lost their way in the forest. By the time we had reformed the procession and had marched a short distance further, it came on to rain with such violence that we were soon soaked to the skin, and were at length compelled to halt. Whilst vainly endeavouring to light a fire in order to obtain some boiled water for drinking, a thunderbolt fell and burst with a loud noise within two or three yards of the spot where we were sitting. No damage, however, was done. The rain having somewhat abated, we moved on again, and after another hour halted about a quarter of a mile from a walled village, beneath the shadow of a large tree. Here we succeeded in lighting a fire and obtaining sufficient boiled water to replenish our bottles. As we were leaving, or rather preparing to do so, I noticed numbers of people running in a most excited manner towards the village, many of them passing by our tent. On inquiry I was informed that a notorious slave-raider was approaching the place, and might be expected to arrive within a few minutes. As it would have been impossible within that time to transport our luggage into the village, I thought it best to take no notice of the report, or, rather, to await events where we were. My personal attendant, Ellassar, who had stuck to us in many previous emergencies, now came to say that he hoped we would not consider it ungrateful on his part if he ran away when the soldiers of the slave-raider came to kill us! We tried to set his mind at rest on this point, and had the less difficulty in doing so as a rumour presently began to circulate that the report of the slave-raider's approach was incorrect. Whilst we were preparing to start again, some men belonging to the village appeared and claimed one of my porters as their property. It transpired that he was a slave, and that he had engaged himself to me without his master's knowledge. Nothing could be done but to surrender the man, as I was not in a position to use force. A further delay ensued whilst I negotiated with the people of the village for the supply of another porter to take the place of the man they had carried away. This done, our procession set out without further mishap, and when we had marched about five miles more we decided to camp for the night on the bank of a dry river-bed, in the hope of finding water to drink. We found two or three fair-sized puddles, and after disturbing some women who had just finished washing their clothes in the water, we filled our various pots with what they had left and carried it up to our camp to be boiled. Our fire had been lighted by the side of a wall, inside which there must have been a consider-able colony of white ants. Either their ap-preciation of, or their objection to, the heat of our fire caused them to emerge in countless multitudes from a hole in the wall close beside the fire. The person in charge shovelled them into it in such quantities that he put the fire out, and had to relight it. The cooking of our dinner was interrupted by an accident which very nearly brought our visit to Nigeria

TYPICAL HAUSA VILLAGE.

[One enclosure such as that in the foreground often contains several huts.]

to an abrupt end. We had camped inside a native courtyard, which contained two huts covered with a sort of thatched roof. In addition to these there was another hut, the roof of which had partially collapsed. This hut our cook was using as his kitchen. The fire which he lit inside suddenly blazed up till it caught the thatched roof. The heat instantly became so intense that we had to retreat to some considerable distance. One of the remaining huts, that in which our luggage, which contained, amongst other necessaries, three thousand cartridges, was stored, was about four yards distant from the blazing kitchen, and had a similar roof made of highly inflammable thatching materials. Had the roof of the second hut caught, our ammunition would certainly have exploded, and our prospects of reaching the coast again would have been exceedingly small. Fortunately, the roof, after blazing fiercely for a few minutes, fell in, and the walls of the hut sufficed to prevent the fire from spreading. The vultures, thirty-three of whom had been sitting on the wall a little while before, benefitted by our misfortune, as two fowls which had been inside the kitchen were so overcooked that we had to give them to the vultures for their dinner.

Having partaken of the somewhat scanty refreshment which our cook provided as a substitute for dinner, we retired to bed, in the hope of obtaining a much-needed repose.

The account above given, which consists of nothing but real incidents, and has in no way been embellished by imagination, will give the reader an idea of the more common incidents of travel which he may anticipate should he decide to make a tour through Nigeria.

HAUSA HUT.

[Showing two methods of pounding and grinding grain.]

CHAPTER VI

TRAVELLING IN NIGERIA

THE story which is told of one of our English railways, in regard to the death of a certain passenger from old age during the progress of the train from Charing Cross to Cannon Street, is one which the English traveller in Nigeria would be quite prepared to credit, provided only that the scene were laid in West Africa. The traveller whose nature it is to be always, or even sometimes, in a hurry would be well advised to refrain from visiting Nigeria. The natives do not understand what being in a hurry means, and should the traveller succeed, after long explanation, in impressing the native with the fact that there was need for immediate action, the latter would probably think it best to wait till the need had passed away or till the would-be traveller had arrived at a more tranquil frame of mind. Complaints are sometimes made as to the dilatoriness of the officials connected with the English post office. The greatest delay I have experienced in the delivery of my own letters was two and a half years. In this case a packet of letters received from England was delivered to a native postman at Lokoja, with instructions to proceed into the centre of the Sudan and continue to make inquiries as to my whereabouts until he found me. After an absence of rather more than two years the postman turned up again at Lokoja to say that his inquiries had proved fruitless and that he had brought back the letters entrusted to him. He further demanded that a sum of thirty shillings, or its equivalent in native goods, should be paid to him to recompense him for the two years' search which he had prosecuted. The letters were finally delivered to me in Ripon by one of Her Majesty's recognised postmen.

It is hard to suggest any single point of resemblance between a walking tour in Eng-

land and one in the interior of West Africa.
Apart from the fact that in either case the
traveller proceeds on foot, the conditions of
travel are as unlike as can well be conceived.
The purse which the traveller in England
would carry with him would weigh perhaps
half a pound ; mine in Nigeria weighed three
thousand five hundred pounds. The weight
of the traveller's purse is due to the fact
that throughout a great part of Nigeria money
in the shape of coins does not exist. The
only money universally recognised consists of
cowry shells and slaves. The value of the
latter is about 150,000 times as great as the
former ; either can be exchanged for their
value in goods or food at every town and
village in Nigeria. The European traveller
who objects to trade in slaves is compelled
to make a very large use of cowry shells.
The cowry shell,[1] *Cypraea moneta*, is used
as money in several different parts of the
world. It was formerly used in Bengal, and
is still accepted in Siam and in Further India.

[1] See illustration p. 56.

The shells are found in shallow water in different parts of the Indian Ocean, especially off the coast of Zanzibar, the Maldive Islands, Ceylon, and Malabar. The chief objection to their use in West Africa is their abundance and their weight, the latter characteristic being of course the result of the former. If one goes out shopping and wishes to purchase goods to the value of an English sovereign, the weight of the necessary cowry shells would be two hundred pounds, or three men's loads. Still worse, if the traveller carries cowry shells along with him for any considerable distance, say two hundred miles, he will find, on his arrival at his destination, that he owes to his porters all the shells that they have been carrying for him and a great many more in addition. To avoid this difficulty he takes with him a large supply of barter goods, especially cloth and silk, a portion of which he exchanges for cowry shells at the different markets at which he stops.

To pass on from native money to that for which native money is most in request, namely, native food. Scarcely any single article of food to which the traveller in England is accustomed would he be likely to meet with there. Moreover, as throughout a considerable part of the country all luggage has to be carried on the heads of porters, it is impossible to take any quantity of English food. The traveller must perforce content himself with the food of the country. The commonest food of all, and that on which the Hausas practically subsist, is a species of millet, to which the name *guinea corn* is often applied. It is found in nearly all parts of Africa and in the West Indies. It has a small scarlet grain not much larger than a pin's head, and grows to a height of six feet. The grain is ground up by the natives and, mixed with a little water, forms a sort of porridge. The chief objection to it is its sour, insipid taste. It is, in fact, so unpalatable that one requires to be very hungry indeed to eat it at all. The natives, however, are not troubled with this difficulty, as they are accustomed to mix with it such large quantities

of red pepper that the taste of the food,
which forms the basis for the red pepper,
becomes a matter of no moment. The traveller who is meditating a visit to Nigeria is
recommended to live, say for a month before
starting, on various sorts of unpalatable food,
mixing with them so much red pepper as to
render the different kinds indistinguishable.
The Hausas say that the reason why they
excel in strength all the neighbouring tribes
is that whereas the others feed on yams or
bananas, they themselves live on guinea corn.
It is not always that the traveller is fortunate
enough to be able to obtain a supply of
guinea corn. He is sometimes reduced to
sweet potatoes and *nuts*. Of the latter there
is an inexhaustible supply in most parts of
the country. A sort of diminutive market
is constantly to be seen under a shady tree
by the side of the path, the ordinary ground
nut being that most commonly on sale. In
the neighbourhood of the rivers Niger and
Binué, and at a few specially favoured places
in the interior, either *plantains* or *bananas*

are to be obtained. The usual plan is to cut the bananas in half and then fry them in palm oil, that is the thick yellow oil which is used on most of our English railways and may often be seen in the boxes over the axles of the wheels. The oil imparts to the bananas a rich orange colour and in addition a very decided flavour. One great advantage connected with its use is that it helps to make a little food go a long way. It frequently happened that we had half a dozen bananas to supply the wants of our party, consisting of three Europeans. Had we eaten them as they were, they would have failed to satisfy the wants of a single individual, whereas after being fried in palm oil they were as much as three could conveniently get through. Within recent years the banana has become much more common in England, owing to the large plantations of them which have been made in the Canary Islands, from which they are now exported to Liverpool. The experiment of eating bananas in native fashion is thus within the reach of any one who lives near a fruiterer's shop and at no great distance from a railway station.

Yams are grown to a limited extent throughout Nigeria. The traveller begins by disliking them owing to their sweet taste, but after awhile he comes to regard them as a comparative luxury. They are the roots of a slender climbing plant, and vary in length from six to eighteen inches. In the South Sea Islands the yam grows to about six times the size that it does in West Africa, possibly owing to the greater suitability of the climate. The yarn is usually boiled and ground up, though the natives often roast them in the fire as a schoolboy roasts a potato in a bonfire.

The *pawpaw* is found throughout a great part of Nigeria. It is used by the natives, and was from time to time used by us to assist the digestion of meat. It can be used either externally or internally; the traveller may either wrap the meat he proposes to eat in a pawpaw leaf and leave it for half an hour, or he may eat part of the pawpaw

NUPÈ BASKET.

[About two feet high, made of woven grass, used for carrying goods on the head.]

itself.   The fruit somewhat resembles a melon, and is of a bright red colour inside.   When I say that practically everything in the way of meat which we ate in Nigeria had first to be minced, the value of the pawpaw may be more easily understood.   On one occasion we attempted to eat some meat which our cook had declared to be more than usually tender without treating it in this way, the result being that the dinner had to be adjourned in the middle to allow of the mincing machine being sent for.   The oft-quoted case of the English official on the coast who suffered from indigestion, and was rash enough to take an extra-sized pawpaw to bed with him, may serve as a useful warning against the indiscriminate use of the fruit.   When the Englishman's friends came to call him in the morning, nothing but the pawpaw was to be seen, and it was not till they had cut it open that the discovery of the watch and buttons of the late official afforded an explanation of what had occurred.

In addition to the articles already mentioned,

the traveller may sometimes be able to obtain
rice, onions, and several roots and small grains
unknown in Europe.   At Kano, and in the
country round, a small quantity of *wheat* is
grown.   This is made into bread after the
regulation quantity of red pepper has been
added to the dough.   The bread is baked
in cakes the size and shape of an ordinary
bun.   A fire is lit inside a large earthen
pot, and when the fire has died down the
dough is stuck on in patches round the inside
of the pot.   The pot is then covered with
mud, and by the time it gets cool the bread
will be sufficiently baked.   In addition to the
articles of food which would form a vegetarian
diet, the traveller may at times obtain eggs
and fowls.   *Eggs* are apparently never eaten
by the natives.   On my asking one of them
why this was so, he replied that they considered
it waste to eat an egg, because if the egg
were left it would develop into a fowl, and
a fowl was better worth eating than an egg.
As the natives do not eat eggs themselves,
they do not distinguish between eggs that

are fresh and eggs that are stale. In fact,
to judge by their almost invariable habit of
providing the traveller with the latter, it would
seem that, like the Chinese, they considered
the value of the egg to be proportionate to
the length of time it had been kept. On
one occasion when the same set of eggs had
been brought to us three times over by three
separate salesmen, it was only by adopting
the method common in England on electioneer-
ing occasions,—viz., by throwing them violently
at the salesman's head,—that we succeeded in
proving that they were unfit for our use.
The difficulty of obtaining fresh eggs is common to all parts of tropical Africa. Her
Majesty's representative at Zanzibar told me
that it was never possible to obtain them
there without the assistance of a man-of-war.
Whenever such visited Zanzibar, the demand
for eggs became so great that within a few
days every bad egg in the neighbourhood
had been sold to the ship's cook. He could
then purchase with confidence any egg that
was brought to him, knowing that it must

have been laid within a few hours. *Fowls* are fairly abundant in Nigeria ; but though their bones are the same in number and size as those of European fowls, they are so diminutive that one fowl will frequently fail to satisfy a hungry traveller. Fortunately the price is not more than a twentieth part of that common in England. Possibly the low quality of African eggs has something to do with the character of the fowls from which they are obtained or of the climate in which the eggs are laid. I have heard, but cannot guarantee the accuracy of the statement, that in a certain district to the north of Nigeria the heat is so great that the inhabitants have been reduced to putting their hens to lay their eggs in ice chests, in order to prevent them from laying hard-boiled eggs.

Besides fowls, cattle, goats, and occasionally sheep, are obtainable in the market attached to any large town. The Hausas also eat the protopterus, or *mudfish*. It is found buried in the mud of many of the West African rivers, and its flesh is regarded as a great

delicacy.   Its length is about three feet.
During the wet season it secretes fat in its
tail sufficient to supply itself with nourishment
during the five or six months of the dry
season.   At the approach of the dry season
it buries itself, forming a regular chamber in
the mud, which it lines with a protecting coat
of hardened mucus.   When the rainy season
returns, it takes to the water again.   The
use which it makes of its tail is analogous
to the use which the camel is said to make
of its hump during its long marches across
the deserts.   The Hausa name for this fish
is "gaiwa."

Locusts are regarded by the Hausas as a
luxury, but are rarely to be obtained.   Whenever a cloud of locusts is seen approaching
any place, the inhabitants turn out with nets,
brushes, sticks, or whatever comes to hand,
and endeavour to beat down the locusts, which
they afterwards fry and eat.   The cloud of
locusts, assuming that it is not about to
alight, usually passes within four or five feet
of the ground, and is perhaps thirty feet thick.

It covers four hundred acres or more at a time, and darkens the whole face of the sky. Fortunately plagues of locusts are far less common in Nigeria than they are in several other parts of Africa.

Next to the question of money and food, the traveller will be likely to take special interest in the various animals common in Nigeria. The creature of which the largest number of different species is to be found is the *snake*. If the statements of the Hausas themselves are to be believed, their language contains no less than three hundred and forty-three words each representing a different species of snake. It is not, however, the number but the venomous nature of the Hausa snakes which gives them their special interest. My informant assured me that three possess so noxious a disposition that any one who sees them, or on whom they look, will shortly afterwards die, the bite of three hundred of them is regarded as fatal, that of thirty may perhaps be cured, whilst the remaining thirteen are believed to be harmless. If this account be true, it is obvious that Nigeria would be a veritable paradise for the student of snakes. For the sake of other readers, however, who may propose to visit the country, I may say that, judging by my own experience, it is extremely difficult to come across the snakes belonging to the first class, and that, if precautions are taken, the second need cause but little anxiety. In compiling the Hausa dictionary, I have not thought it necessary to include the whole available list.

The python is found in the southern part of Nigeria, and many are the feats with which it is credited. One story is perhaps worth repeating, though the details make it difficult to accept it as having occurred in Nigeria. The python of whom the particular story is related sighted a native retreating rapidly on horseback, and vainly endeavoured to overtake him. Finding that the horse was gaining ground, despite his utmost exertions, he rolled himself into the shape of a hoop, and bowling along over the ground effected his purpose forthwith. The special difficulty of believing this occurrence to have taken place in Nigeria is that hoops and wheels of any kind are unknown in the country, and that the python would therefore have to be credited with more than human sagacity. Moreover, had the python afforded the natives so signal an illustration of the use of a wheel for purposes of locomotion, it is hard to believe that they would not have profited by it.

Another creature which forms quite a distinctive feature of West African river scenery is the *crocodile* or alligator. Quantities of them are to be seen on the Niger and the smaller rivers in Nigeria. Except in the event of the traveller's canoe upsetting or of his being rash enough to bathe or to approach the river in the dark, no danger is to be anticipated from their presence. They are usually to be seen lying half asleep on the mud banks. On the approach of a canoe, the crocodile winks one of its eyes to ascertain whether the traveller is meditating an attack, and on being satisfied on this point relapses into its former somnolent condition. If we are to accept the latest accounts given by naturalists, the crocodile ought to be regarded as one of the most useful of animals, and the ancient Egyptians were not quite so foolish as is usually thought when they showed their affection for the crocodile by embalming it. The *British Medical Journal,* in discussing the advisability of stocking the Thames with crocodiles, says : " That much-maligned reptile the crocodile is, in fact, a friend of man, though he tries—generally with success—to hide a sentiment of which perhaps he is ashamed as a weakness. He is an active sanitarian, his special line being the purification of rivers and lakes. With such a certificate of character before them, perhaps some of our river conservancies may be stimulated to secure the services of a few vigorous crocodiles. With these in our rivers the difficult problem of water purification might be finally solved." The inhabitants of Nigeria have two different methods of catching crocodiles when firearms do not happen to be available. Sometimes they will approach one armed only with a spike sharpened at either end. When the crocodile opens its mouth they thrust this in, holding it upright, and as it shuts its mouth it runs the sharpened ends through its jaws and is thus rendered harmless for the time being. The other method is even more dangerous. Whilst staying for a few hours at one of the stations in the Niger delta, I saw a crocodile hauled up on the bank, which some natives had brought in the hope of selling it to the Englishman in charge of the station. They had found it asleep on a mud bank, and had succeeded in winding a coil of the strong native grass round and round its jaws, until it was impossible for it to open its mouth. After tying its feet against its side in a similar way, they pushed it into the water and towed it round with the aid of a canoe to the station where the Englishman was. He agreed to purchase it on the understanding that they were to be responsible for skinning it, and were to be allowed to eat its body. Its miseries having been ended by a Martini bullet, which penetrated its head just in front of the ear, I watched the process of skinning. Neither of these methods of catch-

GROUP OF NATIVES AT AGBERI, LOWER NIGERIA.

ing live crocodiles can be at all safely recommended to tourists or amateurs.

Leopards are very common in Nigeria, and
are most dangerous brutes to encounter. They
will often crouch in the overhanging branch of
a tree, and spring suddenly upon the unwary
traveller who may pass underneath. As the
leopard invariably springs direct at the traveller's throat, there is seldom time to make use
of firearms, even should he chance to have
such in his hand. Only once had I the opportunity of a personal interview with a leopard,
and its duration was but a matter of seconds.
At the end of a day's march I had gone out in
the hope of finding something to shoot, and
was crawling along on all-fours through a
dense piece of jungle, where, owing to the
growth of the creepers which joined tree to
tree, it was impossible to walk upright. Suddenly a mass of yellowish white sprang across
me a yard or so in front, and long before I had
time to lift my rifle had vanished. Whether it
had judged its distance wrongly or were inno-
cent of any evil intent, there was no opportu-

nity for deciding. The natives shoot considerable quantities of leopards, but no doubt many of them get killed in the process.

There are still a large number of *elephants* to be found in the south-eastern portion of Nigeria, in fact there are probably more here than in any other district in Africa. The natives frequently kill them, using only bows and poisoned arrows. They notice that an elephant has been to a certain pool to drink, and acting on the supposition that it will return the same or the following night, they climb a tree near by and await its coming. They then endeavour to shoot one or more poisoned arrows into it. The elephant, looking round and seeing no antagonist, begins to run away. The native thereupon descends from his tree and follows the elephant, taking great care to keep a respectful distance behind it; for should the elephant scent the man, the native would have but a poor chance of escape. The chase of the elephant may sometimes be prolonged for several days and extend over a hundred miles. At last the poison produces its effect, and the elephant drops helpless on the ground. The native approaches stealthily, and as soon as he is convinced that it is no longer capable of harming him, proceeds to cut out the tusks, which will be worth a hundred pounds or more if the ivory be in a good condition. The one and only hope for the African elephant is that the artificial substitute for ivory which has recently been used in the manufacture of billiard balls may so bring down the price of ivory as to render it no longer worth while to hunt elephants. A few years ago the *hippopotamus* was threatened with extinction at the hands of English dentists. It became fashionable to manufacture artificial teeth from the teeth of the hippopotamus, the result being that the hippopotamus was persecuted and killed for the sake of its teeth, as no one was found sufficiently enterprising to extract the teeth from the live hippopotamus. When, however, the dentists discovered a suitable substitute for its teeth, the hippopotamus rapidly declined in value, and for some time past it has been left undisturbed except by the stray shot of a wanton tourist. We may earnestly hope that what has happened in the case of the hippopotamus may at least in part happen in the case of the elephant, and that the fall in the price of ivory may induce the natives to abandon their highly risky methods of hunting.

On one occasion I was explaining to a native in Nigeria how in our country we had tamed the elephant and employed it as a porter. The native burst out laughing in my face, thinking, no doubt, that this was the best lie he had ever listened to. It is difficult to decide with any certainty whether the African elephant was ever tamed in early times. Hannibal brought elephants with him from Carthage when he invaded Italy, but these were almost certainly Indian elephants. The only instance that I know of in which an African elephant was tamed is that of "Jumbo" who created so great a sensation in England some years ago. In the account of Hanno's voyage already referred to, mention is made of elephants having been seen near the coast in

West Africa. In the Sus country, to the south
of Morocco, the elephant is portrayed on some
of the remarkable rock sculptures. It is also
found in the Roman mosaics and frescoes
brought from the south of Tunis, a specimen
of which is to be seen in the Bardo Museum,
near the town of Tunis. General Gordon,
when governor-general of the Sudan, imported
some Indian elephants to the country south of
Khartoum, in the hope that an attempt might
be made with their assistance to tame the
native African elephant. The experiment was,
however, cut short by the conquests of the
Mahdi and by the death of General Gordon
himself. It would be interesting to know
what has since become of the elephants introduced.

Lions are fairly common, especially in the
south-western part of the country. It is
desirable to keep up a good fire at night to
guard against their approach. One of the
most useful of Nigerian birds, from the hungry
traveller's point of view, is the *crested crane*,
a large bird with a spread of wing of six or

seven feet, and with a fine golden tuft on its
head. Its flesh, however, requires to be
treated with a mincing machine before it can
be eaten with any satisfaction. It is very
common throughout the whole country.
Guinea-fowl, pigeons, doves, and one or two
other small birds are also available as food.
Of domestic animals, horses, donkeys, cattle,
sheep, goats, and in the extreme north of the
country camels are found. Except during the
dry season the goat is the only one of these
which is found in the southern part of Nigeria.
The climate seems to kill them directly. On
entering the country during the wet season, I
took a horse with me which marched one day
and then died. Mules are very seldom to be
met with in the country. The French use
them very largely indeed in the hinterland of
Sierra Leone, and it seems well worth making
an experiment on a large scale in order to
ascertain whether the mule would stand the
climate of the districts which border on the
rivers Niger and Binué. Fresh milk, except
that of goats, sheep, or camels, is very difficult

to obtain.   In the districts where cows are to
be found, they are either not milked at all or
their milk is kept to make into butter or sour
cream.   The traveller would be well advised
to take two or three goats with him.   They
can march quite as far and as fast as the native
porters.

The Hausas possess a very respectable
knowledge of medicine, but are ignorant of the
first principles of surgery.   Nor is it easy for
the traveller, even though he be a qualified
doctor, to do very much for them except at the
imminent risk of his own life.   Almost every
patient has what are called in America " shooting friends."   An American coroner who lived
out West was explaining to a friend of mine the
principles which guided him in giving his
decisions in cases of suspected murder.   He
said to him : " In all such cases I give my decision according as a man has shooting friends
or not ; if he has I give it in favour of the
accused, otherwise I give it according as I
think right."   The traveller in a country like
Nigeria needs constantly to bear in mind the

fact that, should any patient whom he has attempted to treat die, his shooting friends are likely to be a cause of serious trouble.

The traveller's ingenuity will be constantly exercised in estimating the value of the smallest present it is possible to give to the various kings whom he visits. The present which they send him is in every case to be regarded, not as an expression of goodwill, but as the formal demand for a larger present to be given in return. It is necessary to take a considerable assortment of goods, so as to suit the idiosyncracies of the various monarchs. Except when staying amongst the cannibal tribes in the hilly districts to the south-east of Nigeria, I found beads and buttons quite useless for purposes of barter. A missionary at home was appealing for aid to evangelize this or some similar district, and in the course of his address he alluded to the fact that the natives had not yet learnt to value clothes, but went entirely naked. A boy who had attended the missionary meeting in company with his father asked his mother, on his return, whether what the missionary had said in regard to the people wearing no clothes was true. On being assured that it was so, he replied "Then, mother, why did father put a button in the collection?" The difficulty which the boy felt in understanding his father's motive, is one which is frequently suggested to those who have to count collections alike for missionary and for other philanthropic purposes.

CHAPTER VII

THE ROYAL NIGER COMPANY

THERE are very few men, whether in the present or the past, who can claim to have presented Great Britain with half a million square miles of new territory. Probably no one but Sir George Taubman Goldie has provided Her Majesty with from twenty to thirty million new subjects. The history of the Royal Niger Company, of which he was the founder and the governor, is one which reflects honour, not only upon himself, but upon all who have taken part in its work, whether in England or on the Niger. Had it not been for the Company, there can be no reasonable doubt but that the whole, or nearly the whole, of Nigeria would at the present moment be under the protection of France or Germany. What the loss to England and to English commerce would

THE RIGHT HON. SIR GEO. TAUBMAN GOLDIE,
P.C., K.C.M.G., D.C.L., LL.D.

have been if this huge area had been closed to our trade in the same way that the French and German possessions in West Africa are now closed, it is scarcely possible to say. The account of the gradual opening up of the Niger and of the districts with which it forms a connecting-link has often been told. It will not be necessary to do more than give the briefest possible sketch. Though the upper waters of the Niger have been known for more than two thousand years, its mouth was only discovered by Lander in 1831. The terrible loss of life which accompanied all efforts to open up the Niger had discouraged one set of traders after another. In 1877, the year in which Sir George Goldie first visited the Niger, a few firms were carrying on a small and decreasing business. Sir George Goldie had been a captain in the Royal Artillery. He had visited Khartoum and some of the surrounding country, and his object in going out to the Niger was partly the hope of exploring the country between the Niger and the Nile, partly to examine the state of the trading companies on the Niger,

in one of which he had a few shares. Fortunately, in view of subsequent events, he
was prevented from carrying out his first
design. On his return to England he succeeded in inducing the various trading companies to amalgamate. In 1880 the French
appeared upon the scene; in 1884 they were
finally bought out by the English Niger Company; in 1886 the Company obtained a royal
charter, and assumed the title of the Royal
Niger Company. The Berlin Conference in
1885 recognised an English sphere of influence
over the lower Niger, but nothing was stated
definitely in regard to Northern Nigeria. The
result was that French and German agents
made hurried marches through the country with
the object of signing treaties with the Fulah
and Hausa kings, by which their lands were
placed under the protection of one or other
power. In some cases, as I have had the
opportunity of knowing, the European text of
these treaties differed seriously from the native
version. In practically every case the French
or German agents arrived on the scene only to

discover that the king had already signed a treaty with the Royal Niger Company, one of the clauses of which provided that the king should make no treaty with any other European power. The Royal Niger Company obtained in all more than four hundred treaties, the result being that when in 1898 the English and French commissioners appointed by their respective Governments met in Paris, the Company was able to produce treaties covering the whole of the vast area to which they laid claim. From the very first the aims of the Company, and especially of its governor, had been political rather than commercial. They have, it is true, paid a highly satisfactory dividend to their shareholders, but they have at the same time been spending a far larger amount on the establishment of a civilized form of government.

It has lately become fashionable to abuse chartered companies, and to regard them as the very worst agents for opening up a new country. Now that the charter of the Royal Niger Company has been revoked, I should,

like to bear a traveller's testimony to the really
splendid work which the Company has done.
Apart from the service which it has rendered
to the Empire by adding to it a large and
densely populated country, it has greatly bene-
fited the natives with whom it has come in
contact, especially in the lower part of Nigeria.
It has abolished many barbarous practices, such
as human sacrifices; it has considerably decreased the slave trade; it has limited and in
most districts entirely abolished the sale of
modern firearms and intoxicating drink. In
Hausaland and the northern part of Nigeria no
inhuman customs such as are so common on the
lower Niger exist, but here the Company has
tried to restrict the trade in slaves, and has
completely stopped the sale of modern firearms
and of gin. The existence of the Royal Niger
Company has been an almost unmitigated
blessing to the peoples whom it has tried to
govern, and the work which it has accomplished
should go far to dispel the idea that a chartered
company is a concern for making money at the
expense of the people it rules.

From January 1st, 1900, the whole of Nigeria has been governed directly by officials appointed by the Colonial department of the British Government.[1] The Niger Company continues to exist for purposes of trade and commerce, though Sir George Goldie has retired from its direction. It remains with the Colonial Office to carry on and develop the work which the Company has begun. In Northern Nigeria, of which General Lugard has been appointed military governor, our protectorate has been established only in name; indeed, many of the natives are living in complete ignorance of the fact that they are under the protection of the British flag. The justification for raising our flag in their midst is in part found in the benefits which they have already received at the hands of the Company, and it will, we trust, be yet more completely afforded by the action of the Imperial Government.

The boys at the S. Mary's Redcliffe School, Bristol, were asked a short time ago to write an essay on a British colony. One of them wrote

[1] Cf. Appendix II.

as follows : "Africa is a British colony. I will tell you how England makes her colonies. First she gets a missionary; when the missionary has found a specially beautiful and fertile tract of country, he gets all his people round him and says, 'Let us pray,' and when all the eyes are shut, up goes the British flag"! Though missionaries have in no way contributed to the result, it is no great exaggeration to say that the great mass of the people of Nigeria have come under the protection of the British flag with their eyes shut. It is for us to see that when their eyes are opened to appreciate the significance of the raising of that flag, they may have reason to be grateful for its presence.

CHAPTER VIII

MISSIONARY ENTERPRISE IN NIGERIA

THE title of this chapter may perhaps be regarded as misleading, as up to the present no missionary work has been done either amongst the Hausas or in any part of Northern Nigeria. Mission work has, however, been carried on for many years in southern Nigeria, and by the time that this book is in print the first serious attempt to establish a permanent mission station in the northern part of the country will have been begun. Bishop Tugwell, the Bishop of Western Equatorial Africa, has recently started with four English missionaries, including two clergymen and a qualified doctor, his intention being to accompany the party, and to start a mission centre either at Kano or more probably at some smaller town on the way up to Kano. The

attempt to introduce Christianity amidst the
unnumbered millions who form the population
of the Central Sudan is one of quite unique
interest. Nowhere else in the world are to be
found peoples at once so numerous and intelligent who have never heard of the Christian
faith. The fact that they are already comparatively civilized, and that large numbers of them
can read and write, adds greatly to the interest
with which the attempt to Christianize them will
be watched. At the present moment about a
third of the inhabitants of Nigeria profess
Mohammedanism, a third are idolaters, and the
remaining third are halting, as it were, between
paganism and Islam. The Mohammedans have
destroyed their idols, but have so far failed to
induce them to adopt the profession of Islam,
the difficulty in most cases being that its profession would involve the observance of the
Ramadan fast, a duty which they shrink from
undertaking. Amongst the Mohammedans
themselves there is very little of the fierce fanaticism which is so common in the Eastern
Sudan. What little there is is confined to the

Fulahs, who won their control of the country by a religious war, and whose only chance of retaining their authority over the Hausas lies in their appeal to a religious sanction. Up to the present time there has been little or no opportunity for attempting missionary work in Nigeria, partly because of the uncertainty both of life and property caused by perpetual slave-raiding, partly because, notwithstanding the religious tolerance of the Hausas themselves, their Fulah rulers would certainly have put to death from political motives any one who embraced Christianity. It is true that neither of these difficulties have been as yet removed, but their final removal is so nearly in sight that an attempt to start missionary work in the country cannot be considered premature.

The question, however, which will suggest itself to many who know something of West Africa is not whether it is possible to christianize the Hausas, but is it worth while making the attempt. If a census were taken of the opinion of the European residents on the coast, who include amongst their number missionaries,

Government officials, and traders, the latter being the most numerous, it would undoubtedly show that a majority entertained serious doubts as to the advisability of trying to christianize any more natives on the lines which have hitherto been adopted. The argument they would use would be expressed thus : The result so far obtained from trying to christianize the natives on the coast and in the Niger delta is that the thin veneer of Christianity which they have received has made them more idle, more untrustworthy, and, above all, more conceited than they were before. The " missionary-man" on the coast is one to be most carefully avoided by anybody in quest of an honest clerk or a trustworthy servant. The Liberian Christians whose conceit has made them the laughing-stock of the coast, are obviously inferior alike in character and physique to the heathen Kroo boys, who are to be found amongst them, and whom they so greatly despise. In Sierra Leone, the oldest missionary centre on the coast, to be a Christian is synonymous with wearing a tall hat and a black coat and refraining as far as possible from doing any hard or manual work. Miss Kingsley, referring to the results of missionary work in West Africa, says : " I grieve to see thousands of pounds wasted that are bitterly needed by our own starving poor. I do not regard the money as wasted because it goes to the African, but because such an immense percentage of it does no good and much harm to him."

It is impossible to deny that these words sum up the opinion of many residents on the coast who are not themselves prejudiced against the Christian faith. It is, moreover, impossible to deny that there is a certain amount of truth in the charges that are brought against the various missionary societies, or rather against the methods adopted by the societies, working on the coast. I remember sitting on the verandah of the Fourah Bay Missionary Training College at Sierra Leone, with its late excellent and heroic principal, Mr. Humphreys, and watching some of the students walking up and down. The typical student was the man dressed in a long black coat with a top hat, gold watch-chain with

magnificent seal attached, gold-tipped cane and
spotless boots. I, and I think Mr. Humphreys,
were dressed in light flannel, this being the only
material suited to such a climate. The college
is intended not only to train missionaries, but
to provide a general education for natives from
any part of the coast. Clerks educated at this
college are to be found all along the coast and
on the river Niger. About a year later I was
staying on the Niger with one of the principal
officials of the Royal Niger Company. After
expressing his interest in missionary work
amongst the natives, he had occasion to refer
to the men whom the Company had from time
to time employed, and who had been trained in
Sierra Leone. He said that experience had
shown that, although their general education
greatly enhanced their value as clerks, they
were so untrustworthy that he had decided
never to employ another, but to substitute
heathen or Mohammedans in their place. The
reason why Christian mission work in this part
of the world has not been the success which
it might have been is not, I believe, that

A NATIVE OF KANO.

Christianity is incapable of influencing the average West African, but that the training of the natives, and still more of the native clergy, has not been satisfactorily arranged for.

There are four important points connected with the training of natives, and especially native clergy, in respect of which reform is necessary if Christianity is to succeed on the coast. In the *first* place, the use of native dress should be made compulsory. There was at Fourah Bay College, when I was there, one student who had the strength of mind to resist the prevailing fashion, and continued to wear the native dress to which he had been accustomed. I understand that in the Universities' Mission to Central Africa, which works on the other side of the continent, and in the Church Missionary Society's work in Uganda, no native is ever employed in any capacity who apes the European by imitating his dress. It will, perhaps, be urged that many of the natives near the coast have little or no dress of their own, and that the would-be missionary must, therefore, adopt some dress other than that of his own people. The same holds equally true on the other side of Africa ; but the solution there is to supply some modification of the Arab dress, which is generally recognised as suited to the climate, and is more or less known throughout the whole of the continent. The point is of far greater importance than would at first appear. Scarcely anything raises so great a barrier between a native pastor and his people as his adoption of a foreign dress. On the Niger delta, for example, you may see the native teacher dressed in the very best and smoothest broadcloth, with his high hat and umbrella, walking about amongst his flock, most of whom if in England would be arrested on the charge of wearing insufficient clothing.

The *second* point is, that all natives, whether students for the ministry or not, should be taught to do some manual work. Had this been done in Sierra Leone during the last half-century, the prospects of Christianity would be much brighter than they now are. The average " missionary-man " regards manual work as degrading, an opinion for which his

training in the past is largely responsible.
Fortunately, the missionary societies are beginning to recognise that book-learning has been
given too important a place, and are endeavouring to supply opportunities for the teaching of
carpentry and other trades. The Bishop of
Sierra Leone has established a technical school
at Freetown; the Basle Mission has for a
considerable time past made the maintenance
of such part of their work, and the "native
pastorate" in the Niger delta receives a
Government grant for the same purpose. Mr.
Geo. Macdonald, late H.M. Director of Education on the Gold Coast, bears emphatic testimony to the good work accomplished by the
Basle Industrial Mission. He says, "I may
add, from a five years' personal acquaintance
with their work in all parts of the colony, that
much good and lasting work has been accomplished by them, and that I hope to see in
the near future a still further development in
their industrial branches."[1]

The *third* point to which I would refer in

[1] *The Gold Coast, Past and Present*, 1898, p. 329.

regard to the training of a native clergy is
that no one should be ordained until he can
talk fluently some native language. A native
clergyman, who had been educated at Fourah
Bay College, retired some time ago from the
mission station which he had occupied on the
river Niger after spending twelve years there,
during which he had made no serious effort to
learn any native language, nor had he ever
preached otherwise than in English. One of
the natives in the district remarked once con-
cerning the house which this clergyman had
built for himself, that in his country no one other
than a king would occupy such a house. Even
in Sierra Leone, where English is generally
understood, the knowledge of one of the languages spoken by the people in the immediate
neighbourhood might well be required as a
qualification for ordination, as such knowledge
would render it possible to carry on mission
work amongst the surrounding heathen.

The *fourth*, and most important point of all,
is the length of time that ought to be regarded
as necessary for training natives prior to their

ordination as clergy. The length of the course at Fourah Bay College varies from two to four years; the training given in connection with the college or otherwise might with advantage be increased fourfold.

The Universities' Mission, before referred to, has to deal with very much the same stamp of native as that found on the West Coast. It very seldom presents a candidate for ordination to the priesthood until he has been trained for at least a dozen years. After ordination to the diaconate, five or six years is all too short a time in which to test a native pastor prior to his ordination to the priesthood, and yet of the nine native clergy at Freetown the average diaconate was sixteen months. I fully believe that if Christianity is ever to spread in West Africa it must be through the instrumentality of native clergy, and that it is alike impossible and undesirable to establish there a reproduction of our English Church. Just because Africa can never be evangelized except by her own sons, it behoves those who are in temporary charge of the infant Church

to take the greatest possible precautions as
to the training of her first clergy. Mistakes made now will leave their mark upon
the native Church for generations, perhaps
centuries, to come. As an illustration of the
length of time needed to eradicate pagan ideas
from the mind of the West African, the following story was told to me by Her Majesty's
representative at a certain place on the West
Coast. The clergyman referred to was an archdeacon, and had had the advantage of a certain
amount of training at a missionary college in
London. The day on which my informant
attended church the archdeacon was preaching
on the subject of witchcraft, a subject specially
suitable for his congregation, as a belief in
witchcraft causes, perhaps, as many deaths in
West Africa as war and disease combined.
He tried to show how impossible it was for
any one who professed Christianity to believe
in any such thing as witchcraft, and urged his
hearers to abandon their belief in it. The
sermon being ended, the archdeacon gave out
two notices, one of which was to the effect

that he had been feeling very unwell for some time past, and that he had reason to believe that two members of his congregation had bewitched him! He added some severe reflections on their conduct. The worthy archdeacon is still living and preaching on the coast, but whether his real belief as to the effect of witchcraft has as yet been modified I do not know.

The argument most commonly employed by those who advocate the rapid increase of the number of native clergy in West Africa is that it was by setting apart "elders in every city" as ministers and teachers that S. Paul first succeeded in spreading Christianity in Syria and Asia Minor. Those who use such an argument appear to forget that most of these elders were Jews, who may be said to have received centuries of special preparation for the work entrusted to them, and that, if in some cases recent converts from heathenism were set apart for this work, they belonged to races who inherited a force of character and a moral stamina which the West African is not likely to acquire for centuries to come. A mere traveller's impressions are, of course, worth little, but any one who has travelled, as I have, through the districts first evangelized by S. Paul, and has afterwards visited and studied the character of the West African, will need but little to assure him that any argument drawn from the experiences of inhabitants of Syria or Asia Minor cannot possibly be applied to the West African native.

One great difficulty in West Africa is to establish a satisfactory connection between religion and morality. The native is naturally emotional, and loves to sing hymns and to go to church, but when it comes to applying the sentiments expressed in his hymns, or the teaching he hears in church, to his ordinary life, it is often impossible to convince him that a religion which is productive of no results in the week-day cannot be genuine on Sunday. At one of the mission stations in Lower Nigeria a committee of natives was formed to translate part of the English Prayer-Book. Their translation was used for a considerable time before it was discovered by the English missionary, who was my informant, and who had learnt their language, that in the introductory prayer, in which the worshippers ask that they "may hereafter live a godly, righteous, and sober life," the word "hereafter" was rendered by a native expression meaning "in the world to come." The translation, whether accidental or not, reflected the wishes of many who had afterwards used the prayer, and who were by no means anxious to allow their Christianity to have too immediate an effect upon their conduct.

It seems scarcely necessary to point out that if precautions are needed against the premature ordination of clergy for a West African Church, such precautions are still more necessary to observe in regard to the consecration of native bishops. Earnestly as I desire to see a native West African Church, with a complete organization of its own, I think the consecration of a native Bishop, with independent jurisdiction, for several generations to come will be a deplorable mistake. The experiment has been tried, and has failed. Bishop Crowther was consecrated Bishop of the Niger territories in 1864, and was Bishop for more than twenty-five years. It would be difficult to imagine a much more winning and attractive man, or one so admirably suited for enlisting the sympathies of English supporters of missionary work. Moreover, he was a thoroughly good man; the critics of missionary work on the coast have nothing but good to say of him. It is, therefore, all the more disappointing to discover that as a Bishop he was an entire failure. He shared the weakness common to all natives of West Africa—*i.e.* the lack of power to control other natives. This was illustrated again and again, to the great detriment of the Church. When, for example, evidence was laid before him by Government officials or traders that one of his clergy had been guilty of actual crime, his invariable reply was, " I never hear evil spoken of my clergy." Since Bishop Crowther's death two other natives have been consecrated as Bishops—Oluwole and Phillips. They are both highly intelligent and good men. As long as the present arrangement lasts, and they are not given any independent sphere of action, but act as suffragans to an English Bishop, no very serious objection can be raised to their appointment. The danger is that people in England, who come into contact with them and admire their goodness and intelligence, will soon begin to ask why such men who are already Bishops should not be allowed to act independently. Moreover, a demand is already being made that native Bishops should be appointed for other districts on the West Coast. The preacher of the sermon on witchcraft before referred to is one of those whose name has been most often mentioned as a suitable man to make Bishop.

The Roman Church has been prosecuting missionary work in Northern China for more than two centuries. The work has met with a large amount of success, but, notwithstanding this and the length of time during which native clergy have been at work, they have not yet ventured to consecrate a Chinese Bishop. As far as regards self-control and force of character, the Chinese are a long way ahead of the West Africans. Surely, then, the experience of the Roman Church [1] may well suggest a caution to those responsible for the control of the Church in West Africa, lest in their anxiety to hasten the spread of Christianity they should defeat the very object they have in view.

The two English Bishops on the coast—Bishop Taylor Smith, of Sierra Leone, and Bishop Tugwell, of Western Equatorial Africa, are exceptionally capable men, and in view of missionary enterprise the two dioceses are most fortunate in having such men at their head.

Before concluding this chapter I should like to say a few words in answer to the objection so often raised by the European residents on the coast to any further attempt to christianize the natives, on the ground that those who at present profess Christianity are idler, less trust-

[1] The Portuguese Church consecrated a native Bishop of the Congo, who had been educated at Lisbon and Rome, in the 16th century, but never repeated the experiment.

worthy, and more conceited than are the heathen. Such a judgment is generally formed from the intercourse which the European has had with native servants or porters. It is a judgment which I entirely endorse if the average servant or porter who calls himself a Christian is to be taken as a fair specimen of the results of Christian teaching. To regard him as such, however, is to do the missionary a cruel injustice. There are a great many natives on the coast and in Lower Nigeria who call themselves Christians; there are distressingly few genuine converts. For every genuine convert available as a servant or porter there are a dozen who will call themselves Christians, and who have perhaps spent a few months in some missionary school, their profession of Christianity being made in order to ingratiate themselves with the white man or to place themselves on an equality with him. My advice to travellers on the coast in search of trustworthy servants would be to prefer the heathen or Mohammedan to the professing Christian, because a bad religion sincerely accepted, or even no religion at all, is to be preferred to a religious profession which is only a sham. When leaving Lokoja on our long march to Kano I found it very difficult to get the sixty porters that I needed. A man came to me and begged to be taken, assuring me that he was a Christian, and that being such he could not lie or cheat. I at once refused his application, but before leaving Lokoja had the curiosity to make inquiries as to his antecedents. I was then informed that he had just been convicted and punished for stealing from one of the officers of the Royal Niger Company. To judge the success of Christianity amongst the natives by the character of a chance servant whom you may be unfortunate enough to employ is certainly a most convenient method to adopt, and one which is common amongst travellers both in Nigeria and in India, but to any one possessing first-hand knowledge of mission work no test could possibly be more misleading or ridiculous.

There is one suggestion which I would venture to make, and which, if carried out, would, I believe, greatly assist the cause of missionary work. Many people at home who entertain no doubts as to the truth of the Christian faith, and whose lives are directly influenced by their belief, hesitate to support the cause of missions because they entertain grave doubts as to the wisdom of the methods adopted by missionaries, and as to the success of the attempts already made. In some cases they have been informed by travellers, government officials, or traders whom they have personally known and whose word they are disposed to trust, that a serious discrepancy exists between the accounts published in missionary magazines and the actual facts. They want to support missionary work, but they are anxious to be assured that their contributions are used in the best possible way. In such cases it is useless to appeal to the testimony of missionaries on the spot, however obvious it may be that these must necessarily know more of missionary work than any one else. What they want is the testimony of independent men who are not themselves connected with missionary work, but who have taken the trouble to make a careful investigation on the spot as to the reality and success of the work in each particular place. If the two Archbishops could see their way to nominate, say a dozen men, of whom at least half should be laymen, to visit the chief centres of missionary work throughout the world and to issue a report, such a report would command the confidence of many who do not at present contribute to missions at all. The inquiries would have to be made, at least in most instances, through the medium of an interpreter, but if the Archbishops' commissioners were men of intelligence, this should prove by no means an insuperable obstacle. The results of such an inquiry would probably be to show that many mistakes had been made in the conduct of mission work in the past, and that even as regards the present condition of things, some of the stories told by travellers and others were not altogether without foundation. On the other hand, the report of the commission would undoubtedly show that even where the roll of nominal converts was but a short one, work of the most real and hopeful nature had in many cases been accomplished. If capable men could be found willing to undertake this work, and if the necessary expenses could be provided by the Society for Promoting Christian Knowledge, or from some other source, it would be of real help in ascertaining the truth about missionary work, and in promoting the spread of Christianity.

CHAPTER IX

THE HAUSA ASSOCIATION

THE Hausa Association was formed towards the end of 1891, with the object of uniting in a common effort on behalf of the Hausa people all who were willing to cooperate in advancing their interests. It originated in a small but representative meeting, which was held at Charing Cross Hotel, at which it was decided to found an association to commemorate and carry on the work of the Rev. John Alfred Robinson, M.A., a scholar of Christ's College, Cambridge, who had been one of the first Englishmen to realize the importance of the Hausa language, and who had died at Lokoja, on the river Niger, whilst attempting to get into touch with the Hausas. The Association was intended to promote the interests of the Hausas in the widest sense of

THE REV. JOHN ALFRED ROBINSON, M.A.,
IN MEMORY OF WHOM THE HAUSA ASSOCIATION WAS FOUNDED.

the term.   The general committee includes the names of representatives of religious or missionary enterprise, such as the two Archbishops, the president of the Church Missionary Society, and a former president of the Wesleyan Conference ; of representatives of political interests, such as the Duke of Westminster,[1] the Right Hon. Sir George Goldie, Sir Harry Johnston, etc.; of men specially interested in philological research, such as Prof. Max Müller and Dr. Peile ; of representatives of science, such as Sir Clements Markham, president of the Royal Geographical Society, Francis Galton, Major Leonard Darwin, etc. ; and lastly, of a representative of English commerce, Sir Albert Rollitt, president of the London Chamber of Commerce.[2]   In order to promote the carrying out of the objects of the Association, the committee decided to send an expedition into the heart of Hausaland to gather information of every kind in regard to the Hausa people and

---

[1] Deceased since the above was written.

[2] For complete list of the committee and further details in regard to the work of the Association, see Appendix.

country, and, if possible, to commence a careful study of their language. They accordingly inserted advertisements in various scientific and other papers, but after waiting a year they found themselves unable to accept any of the applications received, and in default of any one else the committee asked me if I would act as their representative and devote three years to the study of the Hausa language and people. Leaving England in April, 1893, I went in the first instance to Tripoli, partly in order to gain some preliminary knowledge of the language from the many Hausa natives who are to be found at several points on the north coast, partly in the hope that I might be able to avoid the fever-stricken districts in the neighbourhood of the Niger Delta, and approach the Hausa country from the north, by crossing the great Sahara desert. After spending nearly a year I abandoned the latter attempt, and decided to go *via* the river Niger. Since my first visit to Tripoli and Tunis, the French have sent two expeditions to attempt what I had abandoned as impracticable, both of which, I am sorry to say, have been massacred by the Tuareks in the desert. Accompanied by Dr. T. J. Tonkin and Mr. John Bonner, I went up the Niger and for about a hundred miles up the river Binué, and after a long walk through forest land, of four months' duration, reached Kano. We spent three months in Kano, and shorter periods in various other towns, and eventually returned by a different route, striking the Niger a little above Egga. An account of this journey has already been published.

To sum up in a few words some of the work which the Hausa Association has so far accomplished; under its auspices there have been issued (1) "Specimens of Hausa Literature," published by the Cambridge University Press. This consists of a number of Hausa religious and political poems, reproduced by photography in facsimile, with translations and notes appended. The Hausa alphabet is a modification of the Arabic, and is generally understood throughout the country. (2) A Hausa grammar, published by Kegan Paul, Trübner & Co., with exercises, readings, and a short vocabulary. If the recent sale of the grammar affords any test, there are at present about 500 Englishmen engaged in the study of the language, including missionaries, government and civil officials. (3) A Hausa-English dictionary, published by the Cambridge University Press, containing between six and seven thousand entries, though the number of distinct words would be somewhat less. (4) The Gospel of St. John, translated into Hausa by one of their own Mallams in Kano, and revised by me. This has been published by the British and Foreign Bible Society. Further translations of parts of the New Testament are in course of preparation. In 1897 Cambridge University recognised the importance of the study of the Hausa language in a practical way by appointing, in the first instance for a period of three years, a University Lecturer in Hausa. It is hoped that in course of time Cambridge may form the centre for those engaged in England in the study of the language, with a view to afterwards working in Nigeria. The action of the University was soon imitated by the authorities of Christ's College, who, on receiving the promise of financial support from the Hausa Association, established a Hausa scholarship, open to graduates of the University or others who had passed an examination in at least one Semitic language. Mr. W. H. Brooks, who gained high honours both in the semitic and classical triposes, and who has since spent some time in studying Hausa in North Africa, was appointed as their first scholar. Mr. Brooks has since given most valuable help in the publication of the dictionary. The Hausa Association are desirous of appealing to the English public to enable them— (1) To place the endowment of the University lectureship and the post-graduate scholarship on a permanent basis. (2) To continue the publication of the Bible into the Hausa language with a view of facilitating missionary enterprise. (3) To found a college, probably in Kano itself, for teaching and training Hausa-speaking natives.

I would like to add a few words in regard to this latter proposal. A large sum of money was recently contributed to endow a college to be erected at Khartum in memory of General Gordon, its object being to give the natives in their own language an education which might help to raise them out of their former illiterate condition, and to combine with this a course of technical instruction which would be of directly practical use. Kano is a city of immeasurably greater importance than Khartum. Ere very long there will be an English Resident stationed there; the first body of missionaries has already started in the hope of reaching the city. If sufficient money could be raised, not necessarily to endow a college, but to support it from year to year, it might and would exercise a wide-reaching influence throughout the central Sudan. In the case of the Khartum college, the fierce fanaticism of the Mohammedan population was rightly or wrongly regarded as a reason for excluding any Christian teaching from the proposed course of study. In Kano there is little or no religious fanaticism; and although the college would not be a mis-

GUMBO, A HAUSA NATIVE AT TRIPOLI,
IN ARAB DRESS.

sionary institution, there is no reason why it should not work in harmony with any directly missionary work which might be established in the place. The Hausa Association has been in existence for eight years. The whole of its work, including the expedition to Kano, has so far been accomplished with an expenditure of less than two thousand pounds. Its funds are already more than exhausted. It is for the British public to say whether it has sufficient confidence in the names of its committee, and in the object which they desire to carry out, to entrust it with adequate funds to prevent its present work from being interrupted and to render possible development on the lines suggested.

CHAPTER X

A WALK THROUGH THE KANO MARKET

KANO may claim to possess the largest market place, not merely in Africa, but in the world. The French traveller, Colonel Monteuil, estimated its average daily attendance at thirty thousand; and though I should not have ventured on quite so large an one myself, I do not think that his estimate is very extravagant. Size, moreover, is the least interesting feature of the Kano market. In the first place its antiquity is deserving of notice. The market has probably been held on the exact site where we now find it for at least a thousand years. At the time of the Norman conquest of England trade was being conducted in the Kano market amidst surroundings closely resembling those that we now see. Kano would then have furnished better-made cloth than any to be found in England at that time. The really unique interest, however, attaching to this market arises from the fact that it forms the centre of a native civilization which has been attained with very little aid from outside sources and with none at all from Europe. It is the meeting-place of representatives of almost every tribe of any respectable size to be found in Africa north of the equator.

Let us try and picture to ourselves some of the characteristic sights which would be likely to attract our attention on entering the market for the first time. Emerging from one of the narrow winding lanes through which we have ridden from our house or from one of the city gates, we dismount by the side of the deep pond, called the jakara, which forms the northern boundary of the market place. The pond was probably formed centuries ago by the excavation of the mud which was used to build the city. Smaller ponds in course of formation from a similar cause may be seen in other parts of the city. Part of the jakara is blocked up with a bright green plant (*pistia stratiotes*), somewhat resembling lettuce. The other part of it, which is open water, had better not be approached too closely, as the odour which it emits is neither pleasant nor wholesome. Giving a boy our horse to hold, with a promise of a hundred cowries on our return, we begin to push our way through the dense crowd, many of whom seem to be intent rather on gossip than on trade. The first thing that strikes us is the variety of features, of complexion, and of dress. The majority are obviously Hausas, wearing their characteristic dress made of blue, crimson, or white cloth. Next to the Hausas in point of number in the market are the *Fulahs*.[1] Their haughty demeanour and look of conscious superiority betoken the fact that they are the ruling caste in the country. As we stand still for a moment to study the features of those around us, we are rudely jostled by a Fulah mounted on a richly caparisoned horse, followed and preceded by several of his slaves. He is

[1] See illustration, p. 16.

BROTHER OF THE SULTAN OF SOKOTỌ.

A typical Fulah Face.

perhaps on his way to the division of the market where slaves are sold, to part with some unruly slave or to purchase another. His straight, thin nose, well-cut features, and slender limbs make it easy to recognise his nationality. The next man to attract our attention has what is obviously the Christian cross tattooed on his forehead, and carries a sword with a cross cut on its handle. In appearance he is as unlike as possible to either Hausa or Fulah. His fierce, unkempt look suggests that his home does not lie in the city nor in the haunts of civilised men, but that he is a wanderer who has come from the great desert which begins a little to the north of Kano. He belongs, in fact, to the *Tuarek* race, which is scattered over the Great Sahara Desert, and is nearly related to the Berbers of southern Tunis and Algeria. Many of these had embraced Christianity before the Mohammedan era, and the cross serves as a connecting link with the distant past. Some of the other neighbouring tribes refuse to intermarry with them on the ground that the sign of the cross proves that they are not genuine Mohammedans. Engaged in conversation with the Tuarek is a *Bedouin*,[1] whose light complexion and refined expression suggest that she has come from the north, probably from the confines of the desert. The earthen pitcher which she holds in her hands is a specimen of what are on sale in the market, and which are made in large quantities all over Hausaland.

Proceeding a little further we come across the ubiquitous *Jew*, who is, however, but an occasional frequenter of the market. The man next to him, whose complexion is of still lighter colour and contrasts with the dark skins of all the genuine natives, is one of the small colony of *Arab* merchants, some fifty of whom are to be found in Kano. Their houses are distinguished from those of the other inhabitants of the city by the fact that they are built with two storeys. Another man in the same group might at first sight be taken for a Hausa, but his language,

[1] See illustration, pp. 58, 148.

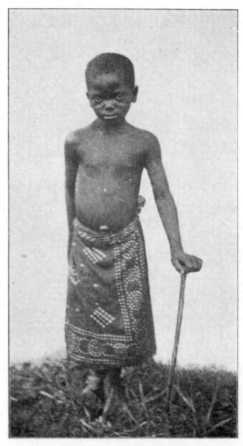

BOY SHOWING TRIBAL MARKS OF A TRIBE
NEAR LOKOJA.

spoken as it appears to be almost entirely through his nose, helps us to recognise him as a native of the *Yoruba* country, which lies behind the colony of Lagos. The tribal marks on the face, which so many of the natives bear, would enable us, were we sufficiently conversant with them, to name the different districts from which the various members of the crowd who are not Hausas have come. For example, the boy in the illustration,[1] with the three cuts running from the top of the nose to a point half-way between the ears and the mouth, is a slave boy belonging to a tribe a little above Lokoja, on the Niger. The illustration of the Nupé girl shows the marks distinctive of the Nupé race, though the Nupés, like the Hausas, are so far civilised that the majority of them wear no tribal marks at all.

Pushing our way through the crowds which encircle the market place, we reach at length the first set of stalls or booths. Some are of a permanent character, built with reeds and mud,

[1] See illustration, p. 36.

and with a low partition dividing the interior from the passing crowd. In other cases the goods of the vendor are spread on mats or on the bare ground, and he is to be seen squatting in their midst. In the part of the market in which camels, horses, cattle, etc., are on sale it is not thought necessary to erect pens, but the owner looks after his property as best he can. We notice that the great market is really made up of a series of little markets, the stalls on which similar goods are sold being grouped together.

We come first of all to the group of stalls where firewood is on sale. Considering how absurdly low is the price of human labour, this is one of the most expensive articles in the market. Coal and peat being unknown, wood is practically the only material that can be used as fuel throughout Kano. Owing to the greatness of the demand, the wood-carriers, who are usually slaves, have to bring bundles of wood or of shrubs from places distant eight or ten miles. They start in the very early morning, and may be seen returning to the city late in the afternoon. A little charcoal is on sale, but owing to its high price is comparatively seldom used.

We now enter the most interesting and characteristic section of the market, which is assigned to the stalls where cloth and ready-made garments are on sale. The natives say that they first learnt how to weave by watch-

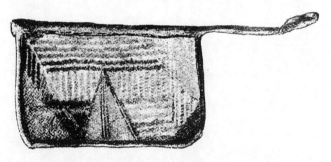

NATIVE FAN MADE OF GRASS.

ing the doings of spiders.   In Kano, at any rate, the knowledge is of extreme antiquity.   Reference has already been made (chap. IV.) to the manufacture of the Kano cloth and the styles of dress common among the Hausas.   In addition to the native-made cloth we notice a certain amount of English cotton goods, which have been brought up from the Niger by native traders. On one fez selling in the market I detected a Manchester trade mark.

Leaving the rows of stalls devoted to the sale of cloth, we pass on to the *leather* market. The principal articles on sale are boots, shoes, pillow-cases, fans, and cases for books.

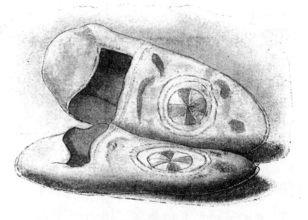

HAUSA SANDALS.

There is also a large quantity of leather, dyed either red or yellow, which has not yet been manufactured. The yellow dye, which is so largely used for colouring the leather, is made from the gambir plant (*uncaria gambir*), a tall shrub which belongs to the natural order

of the rubiaceæ. The plant is stripped of its
leaves and young twigs, and these are boiled
down in shallow dishes. When the juice has
been strained off and evaporated by boiling,
the yellow dye is left. The boots are made so
as to come about half-way up to the knee, and

LEATHER CASE FOR HOLDING A BOOK.

have practically no sole. The shoes, or rather
sandals, are often highly decorated and embroidered. They are carried from Kano all over
the Sudan. The cases for books, one of
which is shown in the illustration, help to keep
the sheets of the MS. together, the art of book-

binding being unknown. The pillow-cases are also decorated with various patterns ; they are intended to be stuffed with the cotton obtained from the silk-cotton tree. The greater part of the leather is made out of the skins of goats, which are very plentiful in the neighbourhood of Kano.

Next to the stalls devoted to the sale of leather we notice those occupied by the vendors of *pottery*. The potter's art has not been developed in Kano to the same extent as many other industries. No glaze or enamel has as yet been discovered. The stalls display a variety of water pitchers, also large jars or crocks similar in size and shape to those used in our own country for keeping bread in. These are intended, not for storing bread, but for making it. A fire is lit inside, and when the fire dies down and the jar is thoroughly heated, the bread is stuck on in patches on the inside and the top is covered over with mud, the sides of the jar being also protected with a layer of mud. In about ten minutes the mud is removed, and the bread is found to be baked. The clay which

A NATIVE OF THE DESERT.

is most appreciated by the potters is that obtained from the ant-hills built by the white ants.

NATIVE KNIFE IN LEATHER SHEATH.

Beyond the pottery stalls come those devoted to the sale of *iron*. The articles on show are of a most miscellanous kind, from swords and

spears down to odd pieces of old iron, the use
of which it would be impossible to conjecture.
The illustration shows a Hausa dagger in red
leather case. Most of this iron is found and
worked by the Hausas themselves. One of
the chief centres of the iron trade is the town
of Fawa, a hundred miles west of Kano. The
furnaces in which the iron is smelted are
about three feet below the level of the ground.
A dozen or more are placed side by side, the
excavation in the ground allowing sufficient
room for the iron, ashes, etc., to be drawn
out at the bottom. The furnaces are round,
and are about a foot and a half in diameter.
The top is left open, and the fuel, which
consists of charcoal made from the shea-butter
tree, is thrown in from above. The ore from
which the iron is obtained is of a light, sandy-
looking colour. The bellows are made in
pairs and require great effort to keep going.
The furnaces are kept alight the whole day, additional ore and fuel being thrown in from time
to time. One cwt. of ore is supposed to produce
nine pounds of iron. The ore is dug out of

the hills in the immediate neighbourhood. In manufacturing the iron into the various articles required, it is usual to make a wax model to begin with, from which a clay mould is afterwards made. Into this mould the molten iron

NATIVE BRASS BOWL.

is poured. The Hausas have not yet developed the art of making steel, and one thing which they were always eager to buy from us was steel files. Brass is imported from England in bars, and is worked up into various articles.

The illustration shows a large brass box made from imported bars.

We pass on next to the stalls where the *kola* nuts are on sale. The kola nut is the chief article of commerce throughout the central and western Sudan. Those that we see on sale have been brought some six hundred miles from the neighbourhood of Salaga, at the back of the Gold Coast Colony. The illustration shows the general appearance of the kola fruit. It grows on a tree about the size of an English chestnut. The fruit somewhat resembles a chestnut and is of a brick-red colour, though another variety (*sterculia macrocarpa*) of a much lighter colour is occasionally to be had. It has an extremely bitter taste, and when chewed acts as a stimulant, and will serve as a substitute for food for long periods of time. The nut when picked costs about five cowries, but by the time it reaches the Kano market sells for two hundred and fifty. It has been used by Europeans resident in Senegal, and has been found to be of use in warding off attacks of fever. Within recent years it has been introduced into Eng-

land ; and if the advertisers of kola-wine, kola-
cocoa, and kola-chocolate are to be believed,
its marvellous properties have by no means
decreased as the result of importation. The
" Forced March Tabloid" sold by Burroughs
& Wellcome is the only preparation which
appears to me to preserve the taste of the original. The kola tree is found up to 15° N.
latitude, but above 10° N. it does not yield
any fruit.

Most of the articles of food on the stalls to
which we next turn have been already alluded
to in chapter VI. We pause for a moment in
front of a stall which we notice is kept by a
leper, where various little cakes and sweetmeats
are exposed. They are made of guinea corn,
flour, rice, honey, and several other ingredients,
and have been fried in oil, several varieties of
which are also to be obtained at his stall. The
two of which he sells the largest quantity are
that obtained from a species of ground nut,
and that from the shea-butter tree (*bassia
parkii*). This latter oil is used for many different purposes. It is rubbed on the body as

a remedy for rheumatism, it serves as oil for lamps, it is eaten instead of butter, and it is largely used for cooking purposes, *e.g.* for frying the cakes that we see on sale. The nuts collected from the tree are first of all broken up to about half the size of peas, and are then placed on the fire till they begin to get soft. They are then ground into a brown-coloured paste between two stones, the paste being afterwards boiled in water. The oil, which rises to the surface, is skimmed off, and is then re-boiled in order to purify it, a white or greenish paste being left about the consistency of lard. The traveller is advised to eat this oil in preference to the butter which is on sale in the market, and which is liable, unless carefully boiled to cause dysentery.

As we go on to another stall we notice that *sugar* and *salt* are selling at about the same price. The former is brought by camels across the great Sahara, and is a luxury only to be indulged in by the rich. The best salt is that which has come up from the Niger, having been imported from England. The native salt, often of a dark-brown colour, has been brought from the Bilma salt-mines to the south of the Sahara.

Soap is on sale at the same stall, though we should certainly not have discovered the fact had we not been told. It is almost black, and forms a paste of about the consistence of putty. It is very scarce and very dear. It

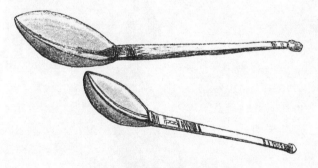

NATIVE SPOONS MADE OF WOOD.

is made from the kernels of the nuts from the husks of which the palm oil is obtained. After the husks have been removed, the kernels are broken up and mixed with ashes. The oil obtained from the crushing of the kernels forms a soap, which though of very uninviting appearance is nevertheless extremely useful. It is chiefly used for washing clothes, as its use in connection with the human body is regarded as superfluous.

FLY WHISK.

Another stall is devoted to a miscellaneous assortment of goods. Wooden spoons, such as those shown in the illustration (p. 155), are used for stirring during the operation of cooking. For the purpose of eating neither spoons nor knives and forks are considered necessary. Whisks, such as that shown, are made of leather and camels' hair, and are in request for keeping off

BASKET MADE OF PLAITED GRASS.

flies. The coarse native grass is used for making baskets, many of which have very pretty patterns.

Leaving the part of the market-place occupied by the stalls, we come to the more open quarter, where camels, horses, and cattle are on

sale. We move out of our way to avoid interfering with three blind men who are pushing
through the crowd, begging alms as they go
along. There are several hundreds of blind
beggars in Kano, who have a king and a regular organization of their own. The lepers,
many of whom we have already noticed moving
freely amongst the other people, also form a
community by themselves, and have their own
king. As I have described elsewhere, leprosy
is terribly common throughout the whole of
northern Nigeria, though it is comparatively
rare in the southern part. The illustration shows
the disfigurement produced by the disease,
which is at least in many cases more dreadful
to look at than painful.

Entering the *camel* market, we find that
business is brisker than usual owing to the
fact that a caravan consisting of over a hundred camels arrived two days ago, having
come across the desert from Tripoli. The
camels that we actually see have only come
from Ghadamis, a distance of about twelve
hundred miles, as the camels which can go, as

A LEPER, LOWER NIGER.

these can, for a week or more at a time without a drink are never taken up to the coast, for fear the moist air should injure them. Kano is the most southerly point to which the camels come. The camels which we see will probably be employed to make the return journey to Ghadamis after they have been allowed about two months in which to recruit. This particular caravan has taken five months on its way from Ghadamis or seven months from Tripoli. This is slightly above the average time occupied. The *horses*, of which there are a large supply, are lean, but they seem active and hardy. Many of them have the blood of Arab ancestors in their veins. They are used chiefly for war and for riding by well-to-do people, and are seldom used for carrying loads. This work is left to the *donkeys*, a large variety of which are on sale close by. Some of them are magnificent specimens of what an ass should be, but the majority show only too plainly by their sore backs and their projecting ribs that they have been both overworked and underfed. From the donkey market we pass to the *cattle* market. We notice that those in charge of the cattle are all Fulahs. There are very few cows, but some fine specimens of oxen with wide extending horns are on sale. These are mostly bought by rich persons who wish to make a feast for their friends, or by those who want to give a present to the king, or some official of importance.

Retracing our steps through the rows of stalls which we have already examined, we come to that which to a European is the most distressing place in Kano—*the slave market.* The usual number of slaves on sale is five hundred. To-day, however, this number has been largely increased, as the king has recently returned bringing with him a thousand new slaves, the result of a month's raiding in the southern part of the territory over which he himself rules. After selecting the nicest-looking slaves for his personal use and presenting a certain number to his friends, he has sent the rest to the market to be sold for his benefit. We have thus the opportunity of comparing the appearance of those who have just been reduced to slavery with those who have been sold and resold and have

been carried far from their original homes.
One or two of the former still wear chains
attached to their hands or feet, but in most
cases this has not been regarded by the owners
as necessary, owing to the extreme difficulty
which a slave would have in escaping even if
he could get clear of the market or the city. Sitting, or rather crouching, in the front row are
several young children, with a look of terror and
misery on their faces ; their fathers were probably killed in the midnight raid upon their
village ; their mothers have been separated from
them for ever and have perhaps gone to swell
the harem of the king or one of his ministers.
One or two of them are apparently too young
to realize what has happened, and are playing
and laughing together.   Of the older slaves belonging to the same group, some have a look of
despair which is more piteous to see than
the most acute misery ; they are under no illu-
sions, but know full well what slavery will mean
to them ; their free, happy life has been exchanged for uncertainty, ill-treatment, and un-
happiness, from which nothing but death will

ever set them free. Others have a look of hatred and defiance in their eyes, which will materially decrease their market value and at the same time will ensure their falling into the hands of some more than usually rough master. A few appear to have already become resigned to their fate. They have owned slaves themselves in the past, and have always looked upon slavery as an evil which might at any time overtake them and which it was vain to struggle against.

Leaving the batch of newly imported slaves, we pass on to notice the others, many of whom have been on sale for several days or even weeks, but have as yet failed to find purchasers. Judging by their variety of appearance and the scars on their faces, at least a dozen tribes are here represented. The most repulsive of those whom we see are not the slaves, but the vendors. If providence intended these men to become slave-dealers, we should find little difficulty in believing the Turkish saying, Every man's destiny stands written on his face. In many cases, if not in all, slavery degrades the master

more than it does the slave, in all cases the
regular slave-dealer sinks lower than his victim.

Some of the slaves we see are obviously of
little market value.   That old man leaning
asleep against the wall would scarcely be worth
his food; that cripple next but one to him would
be of very little use as a porter.   That miserable
woman with her haggard face and her naked
body worn almost to a skeleton, and her small
emaciated babe pressed close to her dry breasts
is not likely to survive long her next change of
masters.   Some of them have been bought and
sold so often that they appear quite careless as
to who their next master is to be, and spend
the time chattering away as though the future
were not worth thinking about.   The expression of the majority suggests a lack of intelligence, and a stolidity, the result of long years
of slavery which has deprived them of all ini-
tiative and would make it impossible for them
to do very much for themselves even if they
could be set free.

Opinions may differ largely as to the de-
sirability of continuing domestic slavery for

another generation in the Central Sudan, but no one who has seen a slave market or has witnessed the actual work of the slave-raider can, I think, hesitate to support a policy which has for its object the forcible extinction of slave raiding and slave markets.

There are several important articles of merchandise which the chance visitor to the market would not see exposed for sale, but which are, nevertheless, usually to be bought if we know where to inquire for them. The most valuable slaves, for example, are never exposed in the open market, but are sold by private arrangement in some of the houses bordering on the market place. *Ostrich feathers* are to be had in considerable quantities; they are brought into the Kano market from the surrounding country, and are generally bought up by merchants who carry them across the desert to Tripoli. *Gold dust* may also be obtained in varying quantities in some of the houses near the market. This is brought by traders who have come from the countries to the back of Dahomey and the Gold Coast.

Captain Binger, who travelled through those districts in 1888, speaks of the large amount of gold obtained by the natives by washing the sands, especially of the upper Black Volta River and its tributaries. It was the exception to come across any one who had not some gold in his possession.

As we turn to leave the market, our attention is attracted to a crowd of people gathered in front of the house which, on inquiry, we learn is assigned to the judge of the market. In a market the size of Kano disputes arising from trade or other causes are of such frequent occurrence that a judge sits throughout the day to try all cases brought before him. As we draw near to the crowd we find that the dispute that is being adjudicated on has arisen in reference to the payment of the brokerage on a camel which has been sold. The custom of the market is that whenever any article changes hands the seller pays to a third party, who is supposed to have facilitated the purchase, a commission amounting to five per cent. of the amount agreed upon. This arrangement holds, not only in the market, but in the case of purchases made in private houses. It sometimes happened that after I had sold, in my own house, some of the barter goods which I had brought with me, after the bargain was, as I imagined, complete, a man would turn up and represent himself as having acted as broker, and demand the five per cent. commission on the sale. The trial affords opportunity for some strong language and correspondingly vehement gesticulation. A pedantic regard for abstract truth cannot properly be included among the virtues of the Hausa natives, and the contradictory evidence produced by the two parties to the suit in question would appear to render the judge's task far from easy. The decision eventually given, based on an independent report which the judge professes to have received, is that the camel in dispute has been stolen from a tributary king a little to the north of Kano, whose tribute to the king of Kano was in arrears, and that the camel would be confiscated to his Majesty's use until such time as the dispute in regard to its sale had been settled and a ransom had been paid by one or other party.

The few stalls which we have visited in our walk through the market form but a very small fraction of the whole number. To write anything approaching a complete description of the great market would require not a chapter but a volume.

CHAPTER XI

THE CAUSE OF AFRICAN FEVER

A S recent discoveries in regard to the cause
of African fever are likely to have a
far-reaching influence on the development of
the whole continent, it will be worth while
giving a brief sketch of the investigations
which have been made into the life and history of the malaria-producing mosquito. It
had long ago been observed that in a large
number of cases of malarial fever the disease
was intermittent; that is, the fever tended to
recur after an interval of two, three, or four
days. Careful microscopical examination of
the patients' blood at length suggested the
theory which has now been established, that
these regular intervals corresponded with the
periods that the bacilli, which were the cause of
the different kinds of fever, took to arrive at

maturity. The development of a large family of bacilli meant a sudden access or return of the fever. The question then arose as to the manner in which the bacillus was conveyed in the first instance to the blood of the human being. An English investigator, Dr. Ross, and the well-known German specialist, Dr. Koch, were engaged in prosecuting researches in malaria, the first in India, the second in East Africa, and arrived independently at the same conclusion, viz., that the source of infection was a certain species of mosquito called anopheles. As the result of a long series of experiments it was shown that the bacillus of malaria was constantly to be found in the head of the anopheles, but in no other mosquito. It was further shown that wherever an epidemic of fever occurred the anopheles was to be found in unusually large numbers.

The subject being one of world-wide interest in view of the thousands of lives which are yearly cut short by malaria, no time has been lost in putting the theory suggested by Dr. Ross and Dr. Koch to the test, and in collecting further information on the subject. The most interesting work has been that done by a medical commission, with Dr. Ross at its head, which has been investigating in Sierra Leone, a place which has earned the title of " the white man's grave," entirely owing to the prevalence of malarial fever. It so happened that at the very time the commission arrived, a peculiarly fatal epidemic of malarial fever was raging amongst the garrison of West Indian troops which is always stationed at Sierra Leone. An examination of the barrack walls showed the presence of several hundreds of the anopheles mosquito ; an examination of the anopheles revealed the bacillus of malaria. The commission proved, beyond reasonable doubt, that the fever had been passed on by this mosquito from man to man, from those who were already infected to those who had before been perfectly well. Whilst gorging itself with the blood of its first victim it had imbibed one or more of the bacilli, and whilst biting its next victim had passed into his blood the bacillus it had extracted from the other.

One anopheles would thus be capable of infecting an unlimited number of persons, the only necessary condition being the presence in the neighbourhood of a single person suffering from malaria. There can be no room for doubt that malaria is capable of spreading from the sick to the healthy, and that it is therefore, in a sense, contagious. The bacilli of all the different kinds of malaria—quartani tertian, and quotidian—have been found in the anopheles, and the result of the commission has been to show that it is very doubtful whether malarial fever can be propagated by any other mosquito or by any other means at all. In view of these discoveries it is obvious that two things must be done : first a vigorous attempt must be made to exterminate the anopheles ; and secondly, far more attention must be paid than has hitherto been the case to the use of mosquito nets. The first suggestion is by no means so impossible as it sounds. The anopheles is distinguishable from other mosquitoes by its size and by its colour. In the course of a very few days

its numbers had visibly diminished at Sierra
Leone, as the result of anopheles hunts in-
augurated by Dr. Ross. A still more effectual
means of destroying it is to search the pools
on which it breeds and to destroy its larvæ.
By this latter method Dr. Ross hopes that
Sierra Leone may ere long completely lose
its reputation of being the white man's
grave, and become, at any rate for residents
on the West Coast, the white man's health
resort. In addition to attempting the destruc-
tion of the anopheles, it will, both at Sierra
Leone and elsewhere, be necessary to take the
greatest precautions against its attack. Wire
mosquito-proof screens should be erected in
front of every door and window. To prevent the entrance of a stray anopheles, double
doors should be arranged to every house.
The traveller on the march, who cannot
use wire netting, should obtain and use the
best possible mosquito nets, and should take
special precautions whilst sitting before his
camp fire at night or walking after dusk.
It should also be generally recognised that

any one who has malarial fever or who has had it within the previous six months is carrying about with him the germs of disease, which only require the aid of an anopheles to pass on to his neighbour.

Whilst the English commission was engaged in investigating the causes of malaria in Sierra Leone, a German commission was engaged in a similar investigation in Tuscany, the marshy districts of which, in the neighbourhood of Grosseto, are notorious hotbeds of malaria. The disease breaks out each year at the beginning of July, when thousands of people flee to the mountains and elsewhere. The anopheles, which was found here in large quantities, can only live with any comfort when the thermometer rises to 80° F. It had been noticed that the sudden outbreak of malaria always occurred three weeks after the hot weather had begun. This was explained, as the result of the investigation of the commission, by the fact that the germ of malaria takes eight or ten days to develop in the anopheles and ten days more to develop in the human being after being injected into him. Outside the human body the malarial germ has never been found except in the mosquito. At the beginning of the hot weather each year the new mosquitoes must therefore get their supply of germs from human beings who had themselves been infected in the previous year. These persons, some of whom have become chronic fever patients, act as a sort of bridge from one year to another. The commission was of opinion that if these patients could be treated with a course of quinine during the eight safe months, they could thus be rendered incapable of infecting the mosquitoes, and so of spreading the disease to their neighbours, and in this way malaria in any particular neighbourhood could be stamped out. They reported several instances in which a localised outbreak of malaria at an inn had been found to date from a period subsequent to the arrival of a traveller suffering from malaria.

Dr. Macdonald, who has been making similar investigations in malaria in southern Spain, has arrived at exactly the same results.

In all cases the responsibility for the spread of the disease has been brought home to the anopheles. In some districts he found large quantities of mosquitoes, but none of them belonging to the species anopheles; in these districts malarial fever was unknown. In all districts in which fever existed the anopheles was proved to be present. Two instances which he cites are sufficiently interesting to quote. He says:[1] "During a four years' residence in a fever-stricken locality, the only Englishman who has avoided fever has invariably slept under curtains. Further, he has always made it a custom, in order to avoid being bitten when sitting outside his house in the evening, to cover his feet with towels, protecting his hands with gloves, and his neck with a muffler. His servant has suffered severely from fever. The only mosquito present in his house is anopheles; they are found in numbers in the rooms of the house and adjoining shed." Speaking of another district, he says : " I visited

[1] *British Medical Journal*, 1899, p. 699.

a fishing colony of one hundred people, all of
whom were suffering from fever at the time
of my visit, for those who were not actually
ill said they awaited their attack next day.
Three deaths had occurred amongst them in
a week. In some stagnant pools close by I
found the anopheles larvæ. The people said
they were bitten furiously at night by a large
mosquito. Their ' patron ' alone slept under
curtains and had not had fever."

The instances which I have quoted from
three different parts of the world will, I think,
be sufficient to prove that the cause of malarial
fever has really been discovered, at the same
time that they afford great hope that the disease
may be checked, if not entirely eradicated. My
own experience is scarcely worth alluding to,
but such as it is, is in favour of the newly
propounded theory. Owing, I presume, to
some defect in my blood, mosquitoes very seldom
troubled to pay their attentions to me, but
devoted themselves to my two companions.
They suffered far more from fever than I did.
Whilst on the march through unknown and

occasionally hostile country, it did not seem safe to envelop oneself in a net at night, so that it was impossible to test the efficacy of such a precaution to ward off fever.

In the course of an address to the Liverpool Chamber of Commerce, Dr. Ross said that he believed that in the coming century the success of Imperialism would depend largely upon success with the microscope. Referring to the return of the commission from Sierra Leone, he said that the immediate object in view was not to banish malaria there and then from the whole continent of Africa, but to ascertain whether there was any chance of exterminating the anopheles from a given malarious area. The conclusion which the commission had unanimously come to was that it would probably be an easy and inexpensive matter to rid Freetown, the capital of Sierra Leone, almost entirely of the anopheles, either by destroying the larvæ in the puddles, or by draining away the puddles altogether.

If it be true, as Dr. Ross asserts, that the mosquito is responsible for most, if not all, cases of malarial fever, it has killed more human beings than it would be possible to reckon. In India alone the mortality believed to be the result of fever is five millions per annum. The bacillus which is the cause of this fever was identified no less than twenty years ago, but until within the last seven years no progress was made towards the discovery of any means by which the bacillus might be destroyed. We can but hope that the next great campaign which England undertakes in Africa will be one waged between an army of scientists armed with microscopes and test-tubes on the one side, and the malarial mosquitoes on the other. Now that the enemy has been discovered, no time should be lost in preparing for the attack. Thousands of useful lives have already been sacrificed in the unequal contest, which, owing to our ignorance, we have been carrying on, as it were, in the dark. War, famine, and pestilence have slain their thousands, but the mosquito has slain its tens of thousands. The successful close of this coming campaign will mark an era in the history and development of nearly half the surface of the globe.

CHAPTER XII

HAUSA WRITINGS AND TRADITIONS

ONE of the most characteristic marks by which a civilized nation is distinguished from an uncivilized one is the possession of a written language and literature. Apart from the Hausas there is no race north of the equator, nor indeed in all Africa, outside Egypt and Abyssinia, which has reduced its language to writing, or made any attempt at the production of a literature. The Hausas have adopted a modified form of the Arabic alphabet, and have produced a number of national poems or songs, besides a limited amount of history in the form of annals and some legal documents. As no other specimens of native literature exist in written form in tropical Africa, it will be interesting to quote a few examples from some of these by way of illustrating the modes of thought of the people. A volume entitled *Specimens of Hausa Literature* has been issued by the Cambridge University Press, consisting of poems, partly of a religious, partly of a political character. They are not of any great antiquity, dating for the most part from about the beginning of this century, one or two of them having been published at the time when the Fulahs were preaching the religious war which resulted in nearly a third of the Hausa population embracing Islam. The poems represent the better side of Mohammedan teaching. There are many passages in them which contain teaching and advice, the adoption of which would have made the Hausas some of the best people to be found anywhere in the world. Unhappily, religious theory and religious practice have as little connection amongst the Hausas as they have so often in our own country.

To quote a few examples of the teaching contained in these poems; the evils of ignorance are described in the most vigorous language.

"Whoever works without knowledge works uselessly.

"The son of the ignorant is a beast and a fool; he destroys himself, he knows nothing at all.

"The son of the ignorant is a corpse even before he is dead; his cunning whilst he is on earth is vain." [1]

The poet's charity does not embrace any outside the number of his co-religionists, thus :—

" I care not for the heathen, he would hear what I say and would pay no attention to it;

" He doubts the existence of pain in the next world; when he comes to the fire he will say, Alas!" [2]

Nor is his opinion of the Jew any better than of the heathen.

" The son of the wicked man is the friend of the heathen, the brother of the Jew; the day is coming when they shall meet with God." [3]

He refers to the various creatures with which he is familiar for illustrations. The ant affords an example of sloth, the cat of insincerity, the ass of stupidity, thus :—

" Sleep not the sleep of the ignorant and careless; he stretches his limbs, he rolls like an ant." [4]

" Repent to God, leave off repenting like a wild cat; it

---

[1] *Specimens of Hausa Literature*, C. 4–6.
[2] *id.* A. 5–7. [3] *id.* D. 29. [4] *id.* D. 27.

repents with the fowl in its mouth, it puts it not
down ;
" He who repents like a wild cat shall indeed have nothing but evil, stripes and chains." [1]
" He (the heathen) would merely lift up his chin and bray
like an ass." [2]

The poet's teaching bears upon the duties
of ordinary life ; amongst those whom he
denounces are " those who sit in the place of
intoxication," those "who steal the earnest
money," the " brokers who have made unjust
profits," those " who regard stealing as lawful,"
" the whisperers of evil." The punishments in
store for such hereafter are most vividly portrayed—" fire shall devour them," " the angels
will lift up bellows, they will increase the fire."
They are reminded of the verse of the Koran
which says : " We will burn them with fire ; as
often as their skins are roasted we will give
them new skins." There are some lines in the
poems which bear a curious resemblance to
passages in the New Testament.

" This life is a sowing place for the next; all who sow
good deeds will behold the great city." [3]

[1] *Specimens of Hausa Literature*, D. 11–12.
[2] *id*. A. 6.   [3] *id*. A. 18.

"Whoever chooses this world rejects the choice of the
next; he seizes one cowrie, but loses two thousand
cowries." [1]
"We have a journey before us which cannot be put aside,
whether you are prepared or unprepared,
"Whether by night or just before the dawn, or in the
morning when the sun has risen." [2]

The impossibility of combining the service of
this world and the next is illustrated thus :—

"Mother and daughter, you choose between them; you
know that you cannot marry them both,
"So too earth and the next world; you know that you
cannot bring them together so as to retain them.
"Look carefully, then, thyself, as to which of them thou
wilt choose." [3]

The uselessness of a merely mechanical
religion is dwelt upon, thus :—

"If there is no purity there is no prayer, as you know; if
there is no prayer there is no drinking of the water
of heaven;
"About this saying there is no uncertainty; whoever
rejects it, leave him alone to become a heathen." [4]

The position assigned to women by the
Hausas contrasts most favourably with their

[1] *id.* A. 39. [3] *id.* B. 26–28.
[2] *id.* B. 55–56. [4] *id.* A. 56–57.

position, both amongst Mohammedan and amongst other native races. This is illustrated in these poems, thus the author of one of them writes :—

> " Farm work is not becoming for a wife, you know ; she
> is free, you may not put her to hoe grass as a slave ;
> " If thou hast not a boy to take her pitcher, do thou
> endeavour to escort her to the water in the evening.
> " And concerning evil living without marriage, God shall
> cause those who live thus to be blotted out." [1]
> " If a woman be in love with two men, they shall suffer
> loss in the next world ; on the day of the resurrection
> they shall rise in the form of dogs." [2]

One of the greatest obstacles to the spread of Islam in Nigeria is the obligation to fast during the month of Ramadan. The tendency to observe the fast in appearance, but not in reality, is sternly rebuked, thus :—

> " He who fasts but at the same time eats in secret, I have
> no doubt but that you may call him a heathen." [3]

Liberality is regarded as one of the greatest of virtues, and its opposite, to which a race of traders such as the Hausas are perhaps naturally

---

[1] *Specimens of Hausa Literature*, A. 24–26.
[2] *id.* A. 33.   [3] *id.* A. 35.

HAUSA WOMAN—MIDDLE CLASS, MOSLEM.

addicted, is threatened with punishment hereafter, thus :—

> "Whoever is stingy, and rejoices in being so, the abode
> of fire shall be opened for him because of his
> stinginess." [1]

The existence of these and other similar
poems, many of which are war songs inciting
people to rise and fight, bears testimony to the
general intelligence, not only of their writers,
but of those to whom they are addressed.
Small schools in which children are taught to
read and write are to be found throughout the
whole of northern Nigeria, the town of Kano containing perhaps thirty or forty. Unfortunately
the Hausa writings as yet obtained afford very
little information in regard to the primitive
beliefs of the Hausa or other peoples in Nigeria.
Mohammedanism has so far interfered with the
early customs of the people that it is only
amongst the less civilized of the Hausa-speaking
tribes to be found in the mountain districts that
we can hope to obtain the information desired.
One of the most interesting of native traditions

[1] *id.* A. 37.

belonging to West Africa is that referred to by Miss Kingsley, as existing amongst the Timné people to the west of Nigeria. According to their tradition, God was very friendly disposed towards men in olden times. Whenever He thought that any man had lived long enough upon earth, He used to send a messenger to invite him to come up and live with Him. One man, on receiving the message, was unwilling to leave the riches which he had accumulated, and refused to accept the invitation which had been brought to him. God, according to the tradition, became angry with the man, and sent another messenger named Disease to summon him. Still the man refused to leave his wealth. On receiving the report of his refusal, God sent a third messenger named Death, and the two messengers, Disease and Death, carried the man off between them. As the result of this man's conduct, God declared that He would never again send His invitations to invite men to come to Him except by the two messengers, Disease and Death. Another West African tradition, in which the same teaching in regard to man's originally happy relationship with God is embodied, comes from Fernando Po, off the mouth of the Niger. Curiously enough, the responsibility of destroying this relationship is laid, as in the Jewish account, upon a woman. The tradition asserts that in early time intercourse between heaven and earth was comparatively free and unrestricted. A ladder was set up from earth to heaven by which the gods used frequently to descend to visit mankind. On one occasion a cripple tried to ascend the ladder. His mother, who was following him, attempted also to ascend, but the gods, being horrified at the approach of a woman, threw down the ladder, and so destroyed for ever the means of communication between heaven and earth. A collection of similar traditions throughout the various tribes of the western and central Sudan would afford invaluable assistance towards the comparative study of African religions. One of the objects for which the Hausa Association has been formed is the collection of Hausa traditions, whether written or oral, and of everything which may enable us to understand better and get into closer touch with their methods of thought.

The native of Nigeria is by no means devoid of the power of reasoning, and will sometimes give expression in simple language to problems which are as old as man himself. The problem of the origin of evil was once stated by a boy [1] on the Niger, who had come under missionary influence, in a most striking form. After the missionary had spent a long time in explaining to him the statement in the creed that God was the Maker of Heaven and Earth, he asked at length, " Did Up-Up make me?" On being told that this was the case, he paused for some time to reflect, and then asked, " Did Up-Up make the buz-buz?" (this being his name for the mosquito). " Yes," was the answer given. Pausing once more for reflection, he asked, " Why does Up-Up let the buz-buz eat me?" It would be difficult to put into simpler words the greatest problem which has ever occupied the attention of mankind.

I was suggesting to a Hausa-speaking native

[1] For portrait of the boy *cf.* p. 143.

one day the undesirability of the permission given by the Mohammedan law to every one to take to himself four wives. The argument which he used was one to which it seemed impossible to suggest any reply. He held up his hand and drew my attention to the fact that God had made it to serve as a pattern of human society ; that as He had united one thumb to four fingers, so He intended one man to be united to four wives.

CHAPTER XIII

PROSPECTS OF MOHAMMEDANISM IN AFRICA

THERE can be little doubt that before the close of the coming century heathenism will be practically extinct in the continent of Africa. The whole population will be either nominally Christian or nominally Mohammedan. It is quite true that in India Christianity and Mohammedanism have for over a century been endeavouring to convert the heathen peoples with whom they have been brought into contact, and that the vast majority are still heathen ; but in India we have at least two different forms of heathenism, with a literature and a culture the result of centuries of development. In Africa, on the other hand, heathenism has never advanced beyond the most elementary and the crudest forms ; in most instances it

NATIVES OF ONITSHA, LOWER NIGER.
Illustrating the rings made of brass or natron worn on the arms and feet.

is a degrading type of fetishism. Long before
the next century has ended, the continent will
be crossed by railways from north to south and
from east to west. With the advance of the
railway, and the consequent progress of civilization, the multitudinous forms of heathenism will
certainly give way to one or other of the two
great religions, Christianity or Mohammedanism.

In trying to forecast the religious future of
Africa, it will be interesting to glance at the
present condition and the immediate prospects
of Islam throughout the Sudan generally. In
the eastern Sudan, that is in the districts near
and to the south of Khartoum, few would be
bold enough to assert that Mohammedanism as
represented by the Mahdi and his successor,
the Khalifa, has had a beneficial or civilizing
effect; but many probably are under the impression that the Mahdists have succeeded in
greatly increasing the number of the nominal
followers of Mohammed in the districts where
they have borne rule and which contain a large
proportion of heathen. If we may accept the

testimony of the man who above all others
would be likely to know the truth, and who was
himself a nominal convert to Islam, Emin
Pasha, the Mahdi's propaganda has been as
great a failure from a religious as from a social
point of view. Speaking of the districts to
the south of Khartoum where he lived for so
many years, he says,[1] " In the last twenty years
Islam has scarcely made ten proselytes in the
whole of the central provinces." A little
further to the south Mohammedanism seemed
likely a few years ago to make considerable
progress in Uganda and the immediate neighbourhood, but the movement by which it spread
was more political than religious; and with the
establishment of a stable government and with
the spread of Christianity in Uganda, it is very
unlikely that it will make any further advance.
In the central and western Sudan it is difficult
to get any trustworthy information as to the
progress of Mohammedanism.   In northern
Nigeria about a third of the population are pro-
fessedly Mohammedans.   In the southern part

[1] *Letters by Emin Pasha*, p. 414.

of Nigeria Islam has scarcely obtained a foothold. In the Yoruba country and in the hinterland of Dahomey, the Gold Coast, Liberia and Sierra Leone, it has certainly gained ground within the last thirty years. In many cases, however, this progress has been due to the fact, that in the constant intertribal fighting the Mohammedans being better armed and more intelligent than the other natives tended to get the upper hand, and so to spread the profession of their own religion. Now that these intertribal wars are rapidly coming to an end, as the result of the interference of the various European powers, it will be interesting to see how far Islam is capable of spreading by mere force of persuasion and argument. As far as West Africa is concerned, Christianity and Islam have scarcely yet come into contact one with another.

The attempt now being made to introduce Christianity into northern Nigeria will be the first serious attempt to bring them into contact. In considering the probable future of Mohammedanism in Africa, it is interesting to notice

that in India, where the same religious toleration prevails as will shortly prevail throughout
West Africa, Islam has made no progress
relatively to the general increase of the population. According to the Government census of
1881, whilst the number of Mohammedans
relative to the whole population had remained
stationary in the greater part of India, in the
Central Provinces it had gone back by about
7 per cent. during the previous decade. It is
true that, in India, Islam is confronted with
religions of a much higher type than it meets
with in Africa; but judging by the rapid
development of missionary work in Africa it
seems likely that the struggle will lie not so
much between Islam and paganism as between
Islam and Christianity, presented as they will
soon be side by side.

I have discussed elsewhere how far it is
likely that there is any great future for the
Mohammedan religion in the world. Whatever the future which awaits it elsewhere, I
believe that in Africa the rôle of Islam is
played out. I would gladly give it credit for

the good which it has done in the past. It has in some districts abolished many cruel, inhuman customs; it has given to some pagan tribes a civilization which they would not easily have gained by any other means; it has given to all who have accepted its teaching a conception of God immeasurably higher than any to which heathenism—least of all the heathenism of Africa—could ever have attained. On the other hand it must be admitted that the progress which Mohammedanism is undoubtedly capable of promoting when it comes in contact with pagan tribes of a debased character, is progress up an *impasse*. Judging by the history of the peoples who have embraced Islam in the past, its spread in Africa amongst heathen tribes would end by placing insuperable obstacles in the very path of civilization along which it had been the first to lead them. Again, to Islam must be attributed nearly the whole responsibility for the great open sore of Africa—slave raiding. There is reason to believe that slave raiding was first developed on any large scale in the

western and central Sudan as the result of the
expedition sent by the Mohammedan Sultan of
Morocco at the end of the sixteenth century; it
is certain that ever since all the worst slave
raiders have been Mohammedans. Once more,
Mohammedanism has completely failed—as far
at any rate as West Africa is concerned—in
enforcing the teaching of its prophet in regard
to abstention from intoxicating drink. In the
hinterland of several of the West African
colonies outside Nigeria where opportunities
for drunkenness exist, the Mohammedans, as
Captain Binger has shown, are frequently the
most drunken of all.

Whilst then we thankfully admit the limited
amount of good which Mohammedanism has
done in the past, we cannot shut our eyes to
its many shortcomings in the present, nor to the
fact that it bars the way to the progress of the
future. There is one country in the world
where Mohammedanism has held undisputed
sway for more than a thousand years. If then
we desire to see the future which Islam would
have to offer to the African native, we need

only turn our eyes to Arabia. A stagnation, moral, social, and intellectual, is the result of a thousand years of Islam. That this condition of things is the direct outcome of Mohammedanism is shown by Palgrave, who had spent a considerable part of his life in Arabia, and had conducted services in mosques on more than one occasion. He says : [1] " When the Koran and Mecca shall have disappeared from Arabia, then and then only can we expect to see the Arab assume that place in the ranks of civilization from which Mohammed and his book have, more than any other cause, long held him back." Unless, therefore, we are prepared to contemplate with equanimity the history of central Africa becoming a repetition of the history of Arabia, we cannot but desire that the influence of Islam in Africa should be curtailed. And in desiring this we are not necessarily making any reflections upon the sincerity of the prophet's religion or of his wish to promote the progress of the world. We may go further

[1] *Journey through Central and Eastern Arabia*, by W. C. Palgrave, i. p. 175.

and admit, as I should be prepared to, that as long as he remained at Mecca, he was a real prophet and was justified in believing that he had received a divine commission. At the same time we may earnestly desire to see his teaching, as explained by his followers of to-day, superseded by Christianity. Moreover, in the very effort to explain the half-truths of the Koran in the light of the Christian faith, and in trying to show to the heathen a more excellent way than that of Islam, we may believe that we are but acting in accordance with the spirit by which at least the earlier part of his own life was inspired, and are doing that which, assuming him to take a continued interest in the history of the world, he would himself desire above all to see done.

[From a Photo by CLARKE, *Cambridge.*

THE AUTHOR IN HAUSA DRESS.

CHAPTER XIV

CONCLUSION

BEFORE closing this brief sketch of Nigeria, it would be well to say a few words in regard to the two treaties recently signed by this country with France and with Germany, by which all disputes as between European powers have been finally arranged. The boundary lines defined by the treaties will be seen on the map attached to this book. It will be sufficient to point out the significance of the principal articles of the treaties. Prior to the agreement of June, 1898, the French had claimed Busa, on the Lower Niger, and had gone so far as to occupy it with an armed force. They further attempted, though unsuccessfully, to introduce gunboats on the Lower Niger. The first five hundred miles of the Niger ascending from the sea are navigable for small steamers, the navigation being then interrupted by two hundred miles of cataracts. The river then becomes navigable again, and continues so for many hundreds of miles. The upper waters of the Niger were acknowledged to belong to France. It will never be possible to open water communication between these and the sea, owing to the existence of the cataracts. It was therefore a matter of little consequence to France whether she obtained an isolated port on the Lower Niger or not, whereas it would have seriously interrupted English enterprise, and have led to constant disputes in the future, if France had maintained the right to keep an armed force in the midst of an English Protectorate, and to introduce firearms and gunboats on the Niger. By the terms of the treaty France foregoes all claims to the Lower Niger, the border between her Protectorate and ours being placed about fifty miles above the lower end of the cataracts.

The treaty provides that for the next thirty

years France is to have the right to lease a
landing place for merchandise in course of
transit, not exceeding four hundred yards in
length, both at the mouth of the river and at
some point further up.

Another question finally settled by the
treaty, and which had been long in dispute,
related to the establishment by one or other
power of a protectorate over Bornu.   The
country of Bornu lies between Hausaland and
Lake Chad.   It has a numerous and intelligent
population, only second to the Hausas in interest.   At the present moment it is under the
sway of Rabbah, the ex-lieutenant of the
Mahdi, who is opposed to all European intervention in the country, and has recently mur-
dered a French expedition which tried to
approach him.   For some time to come we
shall have enough to do to put down slave-
raiding throughout the rest of Nigeria without
attempting to interfere with the misgovernment
of Rabbah ; but it is extremely satisfactory to
know that when the right time comes we shall
be able to include within the Nigeria Protec-

torate the whole of this country, with its immense undeveloped resources, without interference from any European power. On the whole, we have every reason to be satisfied with the treaty which has been signed. We have resigned to France our shadowy claims over vast districts to the north of Nigeria, but have retained all that was necessary to consolidate our own territory.

By a treaty concluded with Germany in November, 1899, the boundary line has been fixed between the German Protectorate of Togoland and our Gold Coast Colony. Although this district does not come within the limits of Nigeria, the trade of Nigeria is so far affected by the agreement that it is worth while referring to its provisions. The most important point is that to England is assigned the entrance to and the navigation of the black Volta, the river which forms the connecting link with the interior. To England has also been assigned the town of Salaga, which is the centre of the kola nut trade, the most important trade of the Central Sudan.

We have, indeed, good reason to congratulate ourselves that frontier disputes, both with France and Germany, have been finally settled, and that the settlement has left to us almost everything that we could reasonably have desired. We earnestly hope that the three nations concerned will now devote the energy which they have spent in disputing over the exact limits of their possessions to developing the resources and civilizing the inhabitants of their respective territories.

There are one or two points to which I should like to refer in conclusion. The first step towards the development of Nigeria must be the abolition of slave-raiding. As long as the majority of the people live in a constant state of fear lest their town or village should be destroyed on the coming night, and they themselves carried off as slaves, we cannot expect any real improvement in the general condition of the country. The marvel is that, despite the existence of this desolating evil, they should have been able to attain so high a degree of civilization. Slaves are used in Nigeria first as porters, and secondly as the currency of the country. During the wet season beasts of burden can only be employed to a limited extent, and even when they are available, slaves are often used by preference. Again, the absence of any proper coinage or substitute for coinage makes it almost impossible to transact business on a large scale, except by using slaves as the medium of exchange. This is especially the case where tribute has to be paid by one king to another. A sort of feudal system prevails throughout most of West Africa, the smaller places paying tribute to the larger. The king of Kano, for example, has two hundred kings who pay tribute to him, the greater part of which is paid in slaves. According to Captain Binger, Samory, whose country lies to the west of Nigeria, pays eight hundred slaves per month for the gunpowder which he receives. Assuming the Hausa-speaking population of Nigeria to be fifteen millions, five millions at the very least of these are slaves. There are probably fifty thousand slaves in Kano itself. On one occasion, after

FULAH HERDSMEN (HEATHEN).

spending thirty-six hours in or on the edge of a slave-raider's camp, and having with difficulty escaped from his clutches, I had to march for four days through country which he had recently raided. In the course of this sixty-mile march, during which we were nearly starved, we passed through village after village destitute alike of inhabitants and of food, the former having been massacred or carried off as slaves by our late host. No one who has not seen a town or village that has recently suffered from such a raid can realize the horror which the constant repetition of such sights from day to day serves to produce. In the presence of this diabolical cruelty and waste of human life, one could not but feel impatient for the day when the forcible intervention of a European power should rid the earth of such crimes. It is quite certain that slave-raiding will never die a natural death. History affords no single instance in which Mohammedans have voluntarily abandoned the slave trade, and Nigeria is certainly not likely to afford such an example. If, then, any excuse were needed for our action in declaring an English protectorate over Nigeria without the consent or even knowledge of its inhabitants, it would be abundantly furnished by the obligation to repress slave-raiding wherever it is in any way possible to do so. England, moreover, has a far higher degree of responsibility in regard to the suppression of the slave trade than any other nation, because England was for upwards of two centuries the greatest slave dealer in the world. Sir John Hawkins, in 1562, was the first Englishman to carry slaves from West Africa to the British possessions in the West Indies. In little more than a century—that is, from 1680 to 1786—it has been computed that over two million slaves were carried across to our American possessions. In the following century the trade developed to a still greater extent. Without taking into account the slaves carried under other flags, it is probable that not less than four million slaves were imported under the English flag from West Africa, and principally from Lower Nigeria, into the West Indies and America. It is impossible for

Englishmen to undo the crimes of the past. What can and ought to be done, and that without a moment's unnecessary delay, is to put a stop—if need be by force of arms—to the trade which we have done so much to develop in the past.

Another subject to which I would like to refer is the much-discussed trade in gin. I believe that, as usually happens in any heated controversy, there has been a great deal of exaggeration on either side. The gin, most of which is made from potatoes and exported in English ships from Hamburg, has been analyzed again and again, and it is by no means the rank poison which temperance advocates have declared it to be. If it were possible to insure that the natives would drink it in moderation, there would be no particular reason for interfering with the trade except on the ground that it tends to oust other and more useful articles from the market. But so far from it being possible to assume the self-restraint of the native, nearly all the evidence supplied by independent travellers in the in-

terior—men, for example, such as Colonel
Lugard and Captain Binger—goes to prove that
an unlimited supply of gin means unlimited
drunkenness and degradation.   Thanks to the
action of the Royal Niger Company, gin is
unknown in Upper Nigeria.   The only two
cases of drunkenness which I witnessed, both
of which were those of professed Mohammedans, were the result of drinking palm wine,
which is more harmful than gin, but which can
only be obtained to a very limited extent.   It
is much to be hoped that the English Government, which has taken over the control of
Nigeria, will enforce the restrictions established
by the Company.   The greater part of the gin
trade, which in many districts has destroyed all
other trade, and which is still on the increase,
is in English hands.   One English trader, who
confessed to me that he had made a large
fortune out of supplying gin and firearms to
the natives in West Africa, complained that he
had been very hardly used because certain
restrictions had now been placed on his trade.
In reply to my suggestion that the gin was

GROUP OF NATIVES ON THE RIVER BINUÉ.

productive of anything but satisfactory results
in the districts to which it was imported, and
that the greater part of his firearms were being
used for the development of slave-raiding, he
said that he understood that the natives who
bought his gin were not yet as drunken as the
inhabitants of the town in which he lived, and
that he could see no reason for limiting the
importation of gin until this stage had been
reached.   In regard to the importation of firearms, he said that if it were true that those
already imported had fallen into the hands of
slave-raiders, this was an additional reason for
continuing the importation, in order that those
attacked might be the better able to defend
themselves.   In view of the proposed construction of railways to connect Lagos and
other places with the interior, it is a matter of
the most pressing importance that an absolute
restriction should be placed upon the carriage
of gin and firearms, lest the railway should
thereby prove almost as great a curse to the
natives of the interior as the slave trade which
it would help to destroy.

"To stamp chaos well under foot and plant wholesome cabbage" has been defined as the rôle which the Englishman is destined by Providence to play in Central Africa. For many years to come Nigeria will afford opportunities on a magnificent scale for the carrying out of these objects. The difficulties which will have to be overcome ere the chaos, resulting from long years of slave-raiding, can be reduced to order, and the cultivation of cabbages or their appropriate substitutes can be developed, will demand much patient toil. The success obtained in India, Egypt, and elsewhere may well afford encouragement to those entrusted with the administration of Nigeria, even though the difficulties to be met with will probably exceed any already experienced. Many a noble life has been laid down in the attempts which have already been made to introduce Christianity and Christian forms of government into the lower part of Nigeria, and the list of those who have fallen, whether as missionaries, soldiers, or administrators, will be a far longer one than it already is ere the desired result can be obtained and our responsibility towards the inhabitants of our latest Protectorate can be in any true sense fulfilled.

APPENDIX I

THE HAUSA ASSOCIATION,

FOR PROMOTING THE STUDY OF THE HAUSA LANGUAGE AND PEOPLE.

Founded in Memory of the REV. JOHN ALFRED ROBINSON, M.A., late Scholar of Christ's College, Cambridge, who died at his work in the employment of the Church Missionary Society, at Lokoja, Niger Territories, on the 25th June, 1891.

GENERAL COMMITTEE.

His Grace The ARCHBISHOP OF CANTERBURY.

His Grace The ARCHBISHOP OF YORK.

His Grace The DUKE OF WESTMINSTER, K.G.

The Rt. Hon. The EARL OF SCARBROUGH.

The Rt. Hon. Viscount WOLSELEY, K.P., &c., Field Marshal, Commander-in-Chief.

The BISHOP OF SALISBURY.

The BISHOP OF WAKEFIELD.

The BISHOP OF SIERRA LEONE.

The Rt. Hon. Lord LOCH, G.C.B., G.C.M.G.

The Rt. Hon. Lord LAMINGTON, K.C.M.G., Governor of Queensland.

The Rt. Hon. Sir GEORGE TAUBMAN-GOLDIE, P.C., K.C.M.G., D.C.L., LL.D., late Governor of the R. Niger Co.

Sir JOHN KENNAWAY, Bart., M.P., President of the Church Missionary Society.

Sir JOHN KIRK, G.C.M.G., K.C.B. Hon. Sc.D.

Sir HARRY JOHNSTON, K.C.B.

Sir ALBERT ROLLIT, D.C.L., M.P., President of the London Chamber of Commerce.

Major-General Sir FRANCIS SCOTT, K.C.B., K.C.M.G., late Inspect. Gen. of the Gold Coast Constabulary.

Sir CLEMENTS R. MARKHAM, K.C.B., F.R.S., President of the Royal Geographical Society.

Rt. Hon. F. MAX MÜLLER, M.A., Professor of Compara tive Philology, Oxford.

Rev. A. J. MASON, D.D., Professor of Divinity, Cambridge.

Rev. J. ARMITAGE ROBINSON, D.D., Canon of Westminster.

Rev. WM. ALLAN, D.D., Bungay, Suffolk.

Rev. J. O. F. MURRAY, B.D., Fellow and Dean of Emmanuel College, Cambridge.

Rev. ARTHUR W. ROBINSON, B.D., Vicar of All Hallows, Barking, E.C.

D. S. MARGOLIOUTH, M.A., Professor of Arabic, Oxford.

Rev. J. H. RIGG, D.D., late President of the Wesleyan Conference.

JOHN PEILE, Litt. D., Master of Christ's College, Cambridge.

FRANCIS GALTON, F.R.S., D.C.L., Hon. Sc.D.

Brigadier-General F. D. LUGARD, C.B., D.S.O.

Major LEONARD DARWIN.

HENRY MORRIS, C.M.S., and British and Foreign Bible Society.

C. HARFORD-BATTERSBY, M.D., M.A.

EXECUTIVE COMMITTEE.

Sir G. GOLDIE, *Chairman*; The BISHOP OF WAKEFIELD, *Vice-Chairman*; Rev. J. O. F. MURRAY, *Hon. Sec.*; Rev. CANON MASON; Rev. A. W. ROBINSON; Major DARWIN; Mr. F. GALTON; Mr. H. MORRIS; Dr. HARFORD-BATTERSBY.

Hon. Treasurer—J. H. TRITTON, Esq., Messrs. BARCLAY, BEVAN & Co., 54, Lombard Street, E.C.

Corresponding Assistant Secretary—Miss CLARK, Arborfield, Weybridge.

The following Societies have expressed their sympathy with the objects of the Association :—

The ROYAL GEOGRAPHICAL SOCIETY.

The SCOTTISH GEOGRAPHICAL SOCIETY.

The MANCHESTER GEOGRAPHICAL SOCIETY.

The ANTHROPOLOGICAL INSTITUTE.

The ANTI-SLAVERY SOCIETY.

The BRITISH AND FOREIGN BIBLE SOCIETY.

The CHURCH MISSIONARY SOCIETY.

The SOCIETY FOR THE PROPAGATION OF THE GOSPEL.

All further particulars in regard to the work of the Association may be obtained on application to the Hon. Secretary, Rev. J. O. MURRAY, Emmanuel College, Cambridge. Subscriptions or donations may be sent to him or direct to the bankers, Messrs. BARCLAY, BEVAN, TRITTON & Co., Lombard Street, E.C.

APPENDIX II

THE following has been translated into Hausa and posted up throughout Nigeria :—

PROCLAMATION.

Be it known to all men that

BY the Order of Her Most Gracious Majesty the Queen of Great Britain and Ireland, Empress of India, the administration of the Protectorate of Northern Nigeria, hitherto known as the Niger Territories, situated between the possessions of France to the west and north, and of Germany to the east, and bounded on the south by the Protectorate of Lagos and Southern Nigeria, will cease from this day to be vested in the Royal Niger Company, Chartered and Limited, and is hereby assumed by Her Majesty. And be it known further to all men that the treaties concluded by the Royal Niger Company by and with the sanction of Her Majesty, and approved by Her Majesty's Secretary of State, will be and remain operative and in force as between Her Majesty and the Kings, Emirs, Chiefs, Princes or other signatories to the same, and all pledges and undertakings therein contained will remain mutually binding on both parties, and all rights, titles and interests of whatsoever nature acquired by virtue of the aforesaid treaties, will be vested in Her Majesty, and all obligations thereunder undertaken by the Royal Niger Company will henceforth be undertaken by Her Majesty. And be it known further to all men that Her Majesty has been pleased to appoint as High Commissioner for the said Protectorate, Colonel Frederick John Dealtry Lugard, Companion of the Most Honourable Order of the Bath, Companion of the Distinguished Service Order. And that the said Frederick John Dealtry Lugard has this day taken the requisite oaths of office and assumed the administration of the said Protectorate, in virtue whereof he has made this Proclamation, whereto his signature and seal are appended this First day of January, One thousand Nine hundred.

HAUSA CANOE

Made by scooping out the trunk of a tree.

INDEX